PHILIPPE VAN WOLPUTTE
TEMPORARY PENETRABLE EXHIBITION SPACES

THIS BOOK IS THE INTRODUCTION OF T.P.E.S. #9
BELOW YOU CAN FIND THE NECESSARY INFORMATION FOR VISITING THE LOCATION

T.P.E.S.9
OPEN FROM
3/7/2015
GO TO
51.231412 N
4.414768 O
KEMPENSTRAAT
ANTWERP
CLIMB FENCE
EXPLORE

Pieter Vermeulen

TRACES OF ABSENCE

Like all big cities, it consisted of irregularity, change, sliding forward, not keeping in step, collisions of things and affairs, and fathomless points of silence in between, of paved ways and wilderness, of one great rhythmic throb and the perpetual discord and dislocation of all opposing rhythms, and as a whole resembled a seething, bubbling fluid in a vessel consisting of the solid materials of buildings, laws, regulations, and historical traditions.
Robert Musil[1]

1 Robert Musil, *The Man Without Qualities*, New York: Coward McCan, 1954, p. 4.

Temporary Penetrable Exhibition Space (T.P.E.S.) is a long-term project that spans over a decade, consisting of various site-specific interventions in the public or semi-public space. The majority of these temporary, ephemeral actions are clandestine or illegal, and have therefore gone unnoticed by many visitors or passers-by. By deliberately blurring the lines between fact and fiction, between genuine and fake, Philippe Van Wolputte creates situations where production and documentation become mutually implicated. As such, they reflect the complicated way in which we use archive material as an access point to invoke a bygone art historical reality, thus often mythologizing its nature. Where does the work begin or end; what are its boundaries? Did the interventions actually take place or are they carefully staged? Are we even able to tell the difference? Can we still 'visit' these historical sites retrospectively, and how does the urban memory work?

The whole T.P.E.S. project is concluded with a solo show at M HKA, where images of its different iterations are put on display. As a final chapter of this long-term undertaking, the exhibition itself is a further articulation of a constant dialectics between construction and reconstruction. Only now, in retrospect, can we start tracing back the origins of this project, in search for recurrent motifs.

Breaking and entering

An apparent motif in Van Wolputte's work is that of the grid. In fact, the grid has been there since the very first T.P.E.S., where it was applied using ordinary white paint and a long wooden stick. After that, we also see installations with spray-painted grids on large plastic sheets. The bluntness of their application and the physical directness of the gesture seem far off from the formal rigidity of the modernist grid, as analyzed by Rosalind Krauss. Krauss argues that, understood in a spatial way, the grid is stating the autonomy of the realm of art. Its overall organization is "flattened, geometricized, ordered, […] antinatural, antimimetic, antireal"[2]. Instead, Van Wolputte's grids are concrete motifs evocating urban structures such as fences and lattices that are used to demarcate and secure certain areas, intended to keep intruders and trespassers out. In several instances, the grid motifs become juxtaposed with the spider-web-like structure of urban maps.

2 Rosalind Krauss, 'Grids', *October,* Vol. 9 (Summer, 1979), pp. 50 – 64.

As the title indicates, most of the T.P.E.S. editions are temporary; not only in terms of visitor access but also due to the fact that the structures themselves will either become demolished or refurbished. In this sense, Van Wolputte's ten-year project perpetually engages with processes of gentrification, always being one step ahead of urban renewal and decay. As most of it has already vanished by now, the remaining documentation therefore becomes a ghostly trace of an absent, bygone reality, a vague memory of what once was.

One of the first T.P.E.S. editions occurred in 2005. Still a student in Antwerp at that time, Van Wolputte intended to create his first "solo show" by illicitly entering an abandoned building right across the campus. The artist entered the building at night, covering all windows with rasterized plastic sheets. Black graffiti at the entrance read "Ingang/ Entrance", "from 18 Oct till 1 Nov / Penetrable Exhibition Space". The text is merely an indicative gesture: it highlighted the building's presence and its accessibility for a limited amount of time. People actually entering the building would find a "list of intruders", again in a kind of grid-like template, inviting them to scribble down their name, signature and date of entering.

Ever since then, several T.P.E.S. actions have been taking place in a wide variety of venues and contexts, ranging from minimal interventions to more elaborately staged settings. For the third edition, which took place in artist-run space Faktor 44 in Antwerp, the idea emerged of creating a base from which visitors could depart in order to locate and discover the actual space.

In 2008, on the occasion of his forthcoming solo show at Wilfried Lentz Gallery in Rotterdam, Van Wolputte decided to "open" a run-down monument not far from the train station. Once part of a large-scale master plan for the renovation of the station and subsequent revaluation of the surrounding area, the structure had soon become a shelter for the homeless. With the gallery as a kind of "outpost" (as it was mentioned on the flyer), visitors were invited to set foot in the forgotten monument.

Another T.P.E.S. was part of a symposium titled *Performing Politics I: Critical Spatial Practices in Art and Architecture,* organized by Eric Ellingsen and Alvaro Urbano at Olafur Eliasson's Institut für Raumexperimente in Berlin (2012). In that same year, Van Wolputte made another installation during the open studios at the Rijksakademie in Amsterdam, where he chose to counteract the typically prestigious event by not opening his studio to visitors. Instead, he made a staircase out of recycled wood leading onto a small and unappealing yard on the backside of the building.

Looking Back While Walking Forward, the video piece included in the eponymous installation at BOZAR in Brussels (2013), also features a T.P.E.S. hidden in a silo in Charleroi. Otherwise inaccessible to visitors, the intervention only survives through this faux-documentary video featuring a group of unidentified characters breaking and entering into an industrial complex.

The last two editions were presented in a more institutional setting. As part of an exchange project titled Het Kanaal/Le Canal, Van Wolputte's work was shown at Extra City Kunsthal Antwerp (in collaboration with NICC) and Espace 251 Nord in Liège.

Finally, the whole T.P.E.S. project is consolidated in a book and a joint retrospective at the Museum of Contemporary Art (M HKA) in Antwerp, where the dark, gloomy images eerily contrast with the brightly lit white cube of the museum.

Where the city is becoming a habitat for an ever-growing number of people, it is also an agonistic site of struggle for space in which several actors are involved: citizens, project developers, property owners, real estate brokers, city councils and such. In an attempt to transform the city into an appealing environment, that is to say, middle-class- and business-friendly, certain parts are intentionally hidden from view. The daily life of most citizens is subject to biopolitical power in a most literal sense, insofar as their bodies are being steered or directed, making only certain zones accessible while obliterating others. The increase in urban monitoring and surveillance, both by police force and technology, is all too often being justified by the delusional belief in the possibility of a public space that can become fully transparent. Just like the ideal of security, transparency is a modernist myth insofar as it relies on neoliberal mechanisms of exclusion and repression[3]. This kind of policy is rooted in a biomorphic illusion of seeing the city as a "healthy body" where diseases and cancerous spots can be cured or removed. Deviant or dysfunctional spaces are situated at the margin of a normalized, disciplined society, and are often also the locus of social injustice, alienation and homelessness. They can function as a refuge for derelicts and misfits[4], the socially deprived living in poor conditions. These dilapidated and decaying edifices, the dwelling places of the Other, so to speak, are often hidden from public view by a façade. This is why the façade, in one form or another, acts as a kind of mask: "The façade comes from a world in which, by using masks well, one clearly separates the public from the private, increases the tension between the two and valorizes the difference."[5]

Of course there are still ways to resist to the dominant, strategic powers that be[6]. Eluding institutional, hegemonic structures of control can be achieved by creating temporary autonomous zones[7]. Occupying and squatting can be seen as tactical ways to reclaim the public domain, as expressions of political protest against market-led housing or as related, socially inspired and anarchist gestures. These are apparent, physical acts of violence, whereby the performers

3 For a philosophical analysis of this "desire for transparency", see Byung-Chul Han, *Transparenzgesellschaft,* Berlin: Matthes & Seitz, 2012. The English translation of this essay is (finally) forthcoming at Stanford University Press.

4 Not surprisingly, *Misfits* is also the title of Van Wolputte's 2014 solo show at Elaine Levy Project gallery in Brussels.

5 Bart Verschaffel, 'Of Façades and Faces' (unpublished in English). Original publication (in Dutch): "Face/Façade: van gevels en gezichten", *Dietsche Warande en Belfort,* 157 (1), 2012, pp. 74 – 83.

can clearly be identified, localized and penalized by surveillance and monitoring techniques. This is what Žižek calls subjective violence[8]. Objective violence, on the other hand, refers to the inherent, invisible violence of a system creating the framework that renders subjective violence possible and that consolidates the status quo of the existing political-economic power relations. Due to its systemic nature, objective violence is less easy to identify or single out. The latter also has serious implications on the level of political framing, understood as symbolical violence. It enables policy makers to reason away the urban inequality and deprivation of certain neighborhoods as self-inflicted, as a result of their own shortcomings and not as the outcome of inadequate policy, discrimination, ghettoization, polarization or exclusion[9]. This perverted line of reasoning often becomes a thankful excuse to justify procedures of urban renewal and gentrification.

The architectural uncanny

Each instance of the T.P.E.S. project installs a sense of disorientation or discomfort, inviting the visitor to leave his or her safety zone. Abandoned areas have always fascinated Philippe Van Wolputte, an interest that could easily date back to his upbringing. His family comes from Doel, a by now deserted village threatened with complete demolition in order to make way for the further extension of the Port of Antwerp. Despite the protest of a large number of inhabitants, the demolition works were started in 2008, accompanied by an unseen riot police force. Still heavily contested, Doel now looks like a war-torn zone and has become a much-favored spot for street artists. In the past years, Van Wolputte has deliberately refused to revisit the place, solely relying on documentation and his imagination, in order to avoid a physical confrontation with its current, depopulated state.

There is definitely something uncanny about this experience. As Freud noted in his 1919 essay, "this uncanny *[unheimlich]* place […] is the entrance to the former home *[Heim]* of all human beings, to the place where everyone dwelt once upon a time and in the beginning."[10] The frightfulness of this experience has everything to do with an unexpected, ghostly return of the repressed, some-

6 French sociologist Michel De Certeau has made the conceptual distinction between 'strategy' and 'tactics': "It must vigilantly make use of the cracks that particular conjunctions open in the surveillance of the proprietary powers. It poaches in them. It creates surprises in them. It can be where it is least expected. It is a guileful ruse." *The Practice of Everyday Life,* University of California Press, 1984, p. 37.

7 Here we can also mention Hakim Bey's anarchist notion of the TAZ (Temporary Autonomous Zone), which has also been an important reference for Philippe Van Wolputte. See Hakim Bey, *TAZ: The Temporary Autonomous Zone, Ontological Anarchy, Poetic Terrorism.*

8 Slavoj Žižek, *Violence,* New York: Picador, 2008.

9 Guy Baeten, 'The Uses of Deprivation in the Neoliberal City' in: BAVO (ed.), *Urban Politics Now. Re-Imagining Democracy in the Neoliberal City,* Rotterdam: NAi Publishers, 2007, p. 49.

thing that was supposed to stay hidden and secret. This "unhomeliness" is brought about by the defamiliarization and estrangement of what was once familiar. The uncanny effect is often amplified by effacing the distinction between reality and imagination. To speak, then, of an "architectural uncanny"[11], would have to be related with a return of the repressed.

As suggested above, our understanding of the urban space is highly ambivalent. On the one hand, the city is supposed to be a "healthy body", monitored by complex forms of social and individual control. In this view, the city would ideally have to take on the features of an ordered, rational grid, a utopian delusion that is fuelled by the desire for power through transparency. On the other, this delusion of a bright, transparent space is doomed to be paired with its other, i.e. obscurity or opacity. In Philippe Van Wolputte's work, these two dimensions – dark and bright, transparent and opaque – are confronted in a complex, dialectical interplay. Inside and outside are mutually implicated, by not only making forgotten spaces accessible but also, for instance, by taking them into the museum.

10 'The Uncanny' (1919), in Sigmund Freud: *Art and Literature*. The Pelican Freud Library, vol. 14, ed. Albert Dickson, Harmondsworth: Penguin Books, 1985, pp. 335 – 376.

11 See Anthony Vidler: T*he Architectural Uncanny: Essays in the Modern Unhomely,* MIT Press, 1994.

Sandra Smets

A MANIFESTO AGAINST INDIFFERENCE

In the vernacular of Rotterdam, a city that is in the habit of bestowing nicknames on objects and buildings, the abstract ornaments from the 1950s that once adorned the entrance to Centraal Station had always been known as the *speculaasjes* (gingerbread cookies). The station's architect, Sybold van Ravesteyn, asked his assistant what it would cost to commission work from the British sculptor Henry Moore. Too much, according to the assistant, so he would take on the job himself. This resulted in what were indeed very Moore-esque, openwork reliefs on the station walls. And as happens in so many cities and particularly in Rotterdam, they were discarded after several decades when the station was demolished. Both the architecture by Van Ravesteyn, the architect whose works would prove to be the poorest survivors in the country, and the *speculaasjes* were considered redundant. Everything had to be newer, bigger, other than it was, once again, and history could be consigned to the dumpster.

Not in the opinion of the artist Philippe van Wolputte. In 2008, he was offered a solo exhibition by the Wilfried Lentz Gallery, which was then located in another recently remodelled building next to the station. Van Wolputte discovered the *speculaasjes* lying on the tracks beside the building site and decided to resurrect them in a new form. He repurposed the sculptures to create shelters for the city's homeless. This Temporary Penetrable Exhibition Space was a social artwork, not only because it helped people on the margins of society - whose community shelters at the station and the Pauluskerk were closed down due to urban development - but also because it gave a new life to a historic relic. But when Van Wolputte removed these pieces to the city fringes, he did not camouflage the degradations of time to which they had been subjected: as with his other editions of T.P.E.S., this one looked dirty, cracked, as though a three-dimensional protest from the punk era.

Knowing this, it is still shocking to look at the photographs that document the T.P.E.S. editions. One becomes the unwilling witness to gritty scenes of decay. These are simply ruined buildings. The black-and-white photography emphasises the sense of filth, bleakness and despair. One would expect to see boldly lettered warning signs, "Enter at your own risk" or "We are not liable for any accidents" at the entrances to the buildings that Van Wolputte invites you to view – but he does so without any warning. His interventions in the public space are invitations to enter buildings that are anything but welcoming. And without wishing to offend the artist, it can feel like a tall order.

These buildings just seem too abandoned, too forgotten. Why should the artist write "ENTRANCE" in large letters on the walls? There are several reasons. His interventions demand that you look at your surroundings with new eyes and employ new ways of thinking about them. Life has been lived in all these buildings: they've seen their share of sorrows and of love. These places are a part of history and contribute to the identity of a city. All too frequently, they are discarded out of a lazy notion of efficiency, of profit and loss, and with all the risks incumbent to such a dogmatic attitude. Cities arise slowly, layer upon layer, and if the past is not acknowledged due to cultural blindness, then people are steering rudderless in a sea of contemporary delusion. Caught up in this delusion are the amnesiac developers and city marketers who dictate how we should value our cities.

The photographs of Van Wolputte swim against this tide since they refer to earlier times. Even though they were taken recently, the pictures look dated, as though from the 1980s. The black writing on the facades could be the names of galleries but have the appearance of illegal and angry graffiti tags. They are signs of protest, intended to break open the city and to reclaim the space that should belong to everyone. Down with walls, fences and private property.

In the postwar years of Van Ravesteyn and his associates, many of the western world's cities were undergoing rapid development. But with the advent of skyscrapers and walls arrived a world that declared that happiness was synonymous with wealth and ownership. Just as Van Wolputte does now, the art world of the time questioned this ideology of expansionism. Artists in various European cities revisited Surrealist plans to explore the city psychogeographically. Using a map of Paris to walk through London, dice to decide which route to take, under the influence of drugs or at night, the purpose was to eliminate the all too familiar and obvious perceptions of a new city. Comfort and luxury was bourgeois and not a serious option, an attitude reflected in Van Wolputte's disquieting photographs of squats.

While his interventions are relatively temporary, the photographs are more permanent. When you record something you save something. Van Wolputte began his visual plea for preservation in 2005, after which the underlying message of the social debate became more urgent. Firstly, there are the many evictions caused by rising mortgages, which while they are legal do not feel ethically correct. Secondly, the speculation and rapacious building boom that is occurring in many cities, including Antwerp and Rotterdam, have drastically increased the vacancy rate of commercial properties. Developers are effectively creating ghost towns.

This does make Van Wolputte's spooky photographs simultaneously an indictment and a proposal: look at things differently, find a way to value what already exists. Not through gentrification, which is a temporary solution to an economic impasse. This is the point he makes by presenting us with photographs that are hardly positive and inviting. Instead they demand that we shake off our indifference to the public space and become more aware of social injustice. Public space should be public, accessible to everyone.

This is how it used to be. Street names such as *Meent* (common land) recall the communal nature of areas where everyone had the right to graze sheep or grow vegetables. The photographs of Van Wolputte show us a post-community world where everything is fenced off and appropriated. Van Wolputte's interventions hack the space and "de-fence". They are a plea for more commonality, where one can imagine the homeless living in artworks and sheep grazing everywhere.

In Rotterdam, he may have won the argument. The new station building, which opened in 2014, is once again decorated with the same *speculaasjes,* and the frieze that runs through the building references the *speculaasjes* motif. The homeless people won a victory too: that year, the new Pauluskerk homeless shelter annex opened, a stone's throw from the station. This version of Van Wolputte's Temporary Penetrable Exhibition Space will no doubt know a greater permanence.

Eric Fredericksen

ZERO LOT LINE
A HOLE IS TO DIG

A solid wall wants an opening. An open field makes no such demands. One pleasure of the city is its constant assertion of boundaries: limits within which the imagination immediately conceives exceptions. In the logical, reversed syntax of Ruth Krauss' great children's book[1], a wall is to find a gap.

To me, the open field wants a wall. In the U.S., where I live, buildings are rarely permitted to run along the property line without setbacks, making continuous street walls uncommon. As such, the almost endless expanses of perimeter block housing in Berlin, to take one example, can seem exotic and wondrous to a visitor from the States—me for example, a 20-year-old student visiting in 1990, hunting for small cinemas or music clubs—especially upon discovering that none of them were accessible from the street, but must be sought inside, in the *Hof*. After the seeker discovers the break in the neoclassical bluff and enters a cave, a second landscape is discovered behind the first, dressed stone giving way to rougher brick and plaster structures in jumbled, illegible layouts. In one, an upstairs cinema playing horror movies, with sofas instead of seats, a bar to the side and cigarette smoke in the air. In a different *Hof*, a basement club where a minor SST band[2] plays sprawling instrumentals. From the street, one could imagine, all this didn't exist.

In other, less porous cities, with tighter arrangements of streets and compressed building lots—Paris for example—the continuous street wall might retain its solidity for long stretches, a regular cliff face with no caverns or grottoes, no springs issuing from deep within. Not for you, at least. Hence the splendors of the glassy storefront to Atget, or the arcades to Benjamin. A visual or physical penetration of the forbidding walls is available to all who pass by or through, even if the visions behind glass remain inaccessible.[3]

The need to find a wall's opening, to discover your own way through the fortification, is not only a natural response to the wall's assertion of property or the segregations a wall

1 Ruth Krauss, *A Hole Is to Dig*, New York: HarperCollins, 1989.

2 Alter Natives. They introduced each instrumental as a different Madonna hit.

3 In the US, this democracy of views was largely supplanted by dispersion of populations across sprawling, economically segregated suburbs. You see what you can't have through a screen rather than a window. Walls, then, are lovely to us primarily because they are clear about what they do.

maintains. The allure of both the wall and its fissures seem more deeply embedded.

Start with the brain within its inescapable perimeter. The bone-white rotunda described in Samuel Beckett's "Imagination Dead Imagine" [4] and the two pale bodies within, a light rising and falling, their breaths alongside. The brain in its skull, and your imagination constructing a rendering of its interior according to the author's schematic instructions, imagining itself (for company). You might feel a strong desire to think your way out of that unyielding enclosure. Generally, in Beckett, you cannot.

Or start in the womb, the original enclosure. Like the wall, so necessary for security and shelter; like the wall, a naturalized limit to activity, a separation of inside from outside, of the personal and familial from the public and polymorphous exterior. Beckett was greatly taken by the psychoanalyst and Freud protégé Otto Rank's *The Trauma of Birth,*[5] which argues that neuroses are driven by the trauma of expulsion from the womb, and attended by a compulsion to return. But for Beckett, who claimed he remembered life in the womb, it was a place of horror. A friend quoted him saying he wrote "out of obligation toward that enclosed poor embryo." [6] Hence the half-buried protagonist of *Happy Days,* the three actor's heads protruding from vases in *Play,* and all the dark rooms and hollows of the fiction.[7]

Childhood fantasies of turning the world upside-down (restoring us to our typical orientation in the womb), of entering small spaces (wardrobes, elevators, police callboxes) and finding in them openings to new worlds—do these suggest a symbolic affinity with Rank's theory? Why do fictional evocations of these inversions and expansions so please us, whether the transformation is monstrous (Gregor Samsa climbing to the ceiling) or fantastic (the entrances through garden walls or wardrobes to Narnia)? Whether one experiences these womblike situations as horrifying or enthralling, they end in disappointment each time we emerge, finding ourselves and the outer world largely unchanged. We have failed again to find the bridge to Terabithia.

4 "Imagination Dead Imagine" (1966) in Samuel Beckett, *First Love and Other Shorts,* New York: Grove, 1974, p. 61.

5 Otto Rank, *The Trauma of Birth,* New York: Harcourt, Brace, 1929.

6 Graley Herren, "A Womb with a View: *Film* as Regression Fantasy" in S.E. Gontarski, *The Edinburgh Companion to Samuel Beckett and the Arts,* Edinburgh University Press, 2014, p. 243.

7 For others, these conditions may seem thrilling. An affinity for close spaces—*a claustrophilia*—connects the dream states attained in isolation tanks, a child hiding in the corner of a dark closet or steamer trunk, or spelunking. These are not pleasures every person shares, certainly, but for those of us who do, the frisson is hard to rationally explain.

8 Richard Hugo, "Statements of Faith" (1979) in *The Triggering Town,* New York: W.W. Norton, 2010, p. 73.

Denied rebirth, we wander the overfamiliar city. It may be overly familiar because it is old, rich and perfected, or, in a rapidly developing city, because new construction everywhere looks like new construction everywhere. We wander to try to find the strange in the familiar: The too-well-known layout of the streets, the technocratic management of transportation systems, the construction methods and economics of the typical building types, the repetitive leisure-class boutiques and restaurants, the rationality and haute-bourgeois economics of the contemporary city, barely alleviated by the occasional interesting civic folly (a new museum, library, stadium, or tunnel). What sends artists howling off into the entropic embrace of collapsed cities or districts whose economic function has been temporarily severed, is only partly economic necessity. Partly it is the need to project an imagination across an open and somewhat stagnant landscape. A city in a frenzy of redevelopment trumps individual imagination with the brash scale of construction.

The Seattle poet Richard Hugo wrote of "the imagination's impulse to create unknowns out of knowns [....] If the knowns keep changing, the process of creating the unknowns is constantly threatened because the base of operations is unstable."[8]

Artists' general impulse to make new things from old does not typically extend to land use and development. "One problem for modern poets," Hugo continues, "is the wholesale changes in what we see—the tearing down of buildings, the development of new housing, the accelerated rate of loss of all things that can serve as visual checkpoints and sources of stability." What is at stake here is beyond economics, it is the imaginative possibilities of the city.

"We are bored in the city" begins Ivan Chtcheglov's Lettrist text "Formulary for a New Urbanism."[9] In the "closed landscape" of the city, "original conceptions of space" can only be found in "certain shifting angles, certain receding perspectives." In between these fragmentary glimpses, "Everyone wavers between the emotionally still-alive past and the already dead future."

9 Ivan Chtcheglov (trans. Ken Knabb), "Formulary for a New Urbanism" (1953), accessed June 12, 2015. http://www.bopsecrets.org/SI/Chtcheglov.htm

"We don't intend to prolong the mechanistic civilizations and frigid architecture that ultimately lead to boring leisure," he writes. "We propose to invent new, changeable decors."

But we are done with visionary urban design: dreams of remaking the city are left to the developers and politicians. Maybe we lifted the paving-stones and found only deserts. That doesn't mean we don't still dream of beaches (caverns, Edens). To find the breaks in walls and spaces behind and occupy them, if only briefly. To uncover something strange within the regularized cityscape. To find the redundant spot, the exception to economic logic; to invite others into a small, empty place where imagination could play for a moment. Just to show that it is possible.

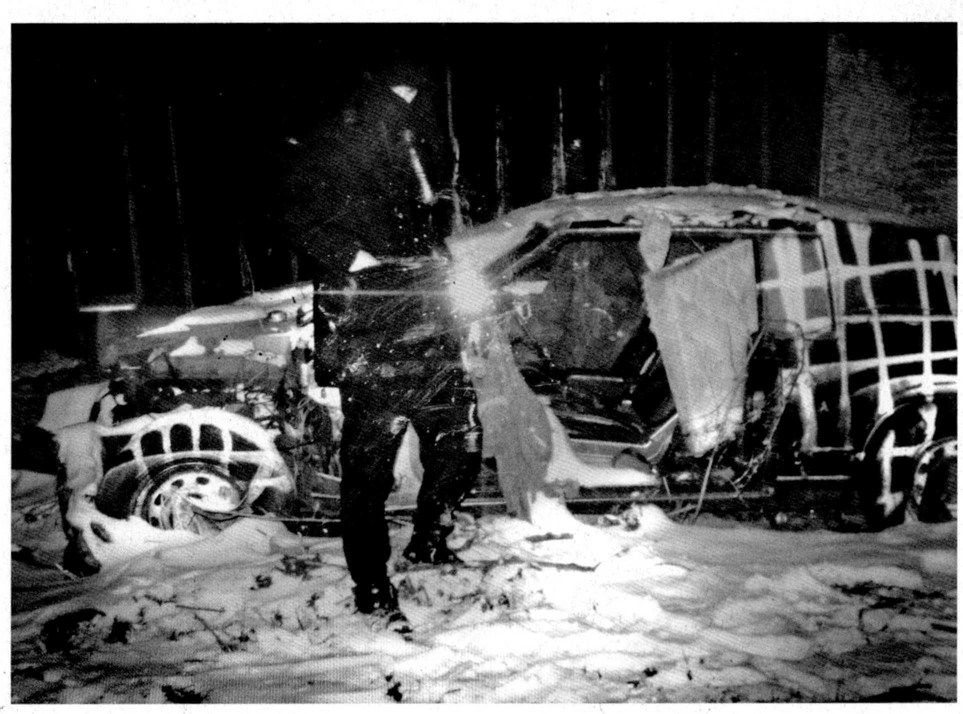

T.P.E.S. 0
St.Jozefstraat 35,
Antwerp (BE)
opened on 02.03.2004

T.P.E.S. 0 (2004)
Intervention at
St.Jozefstraat 35,
Antwerp (BE)

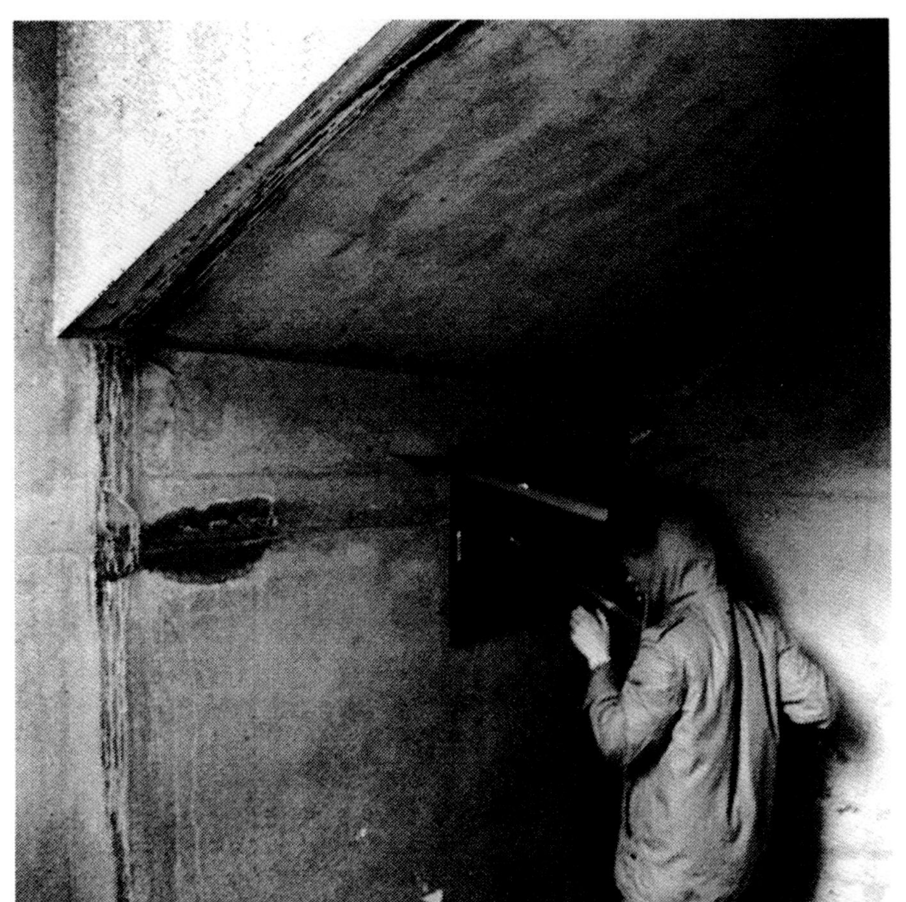

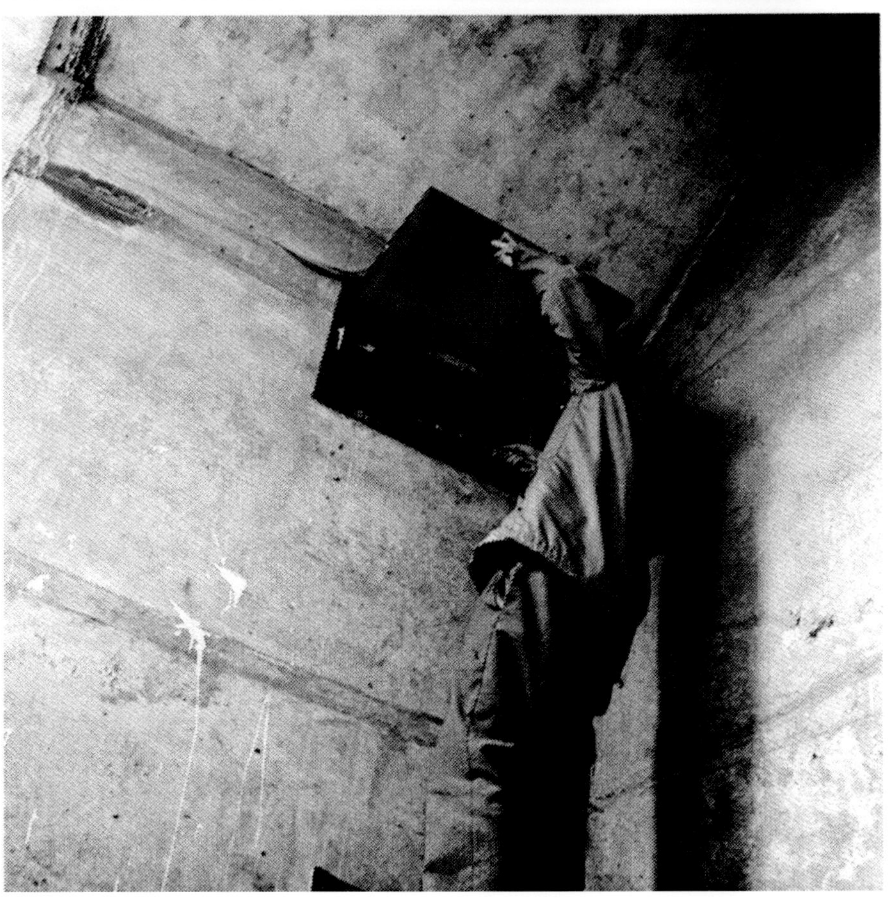

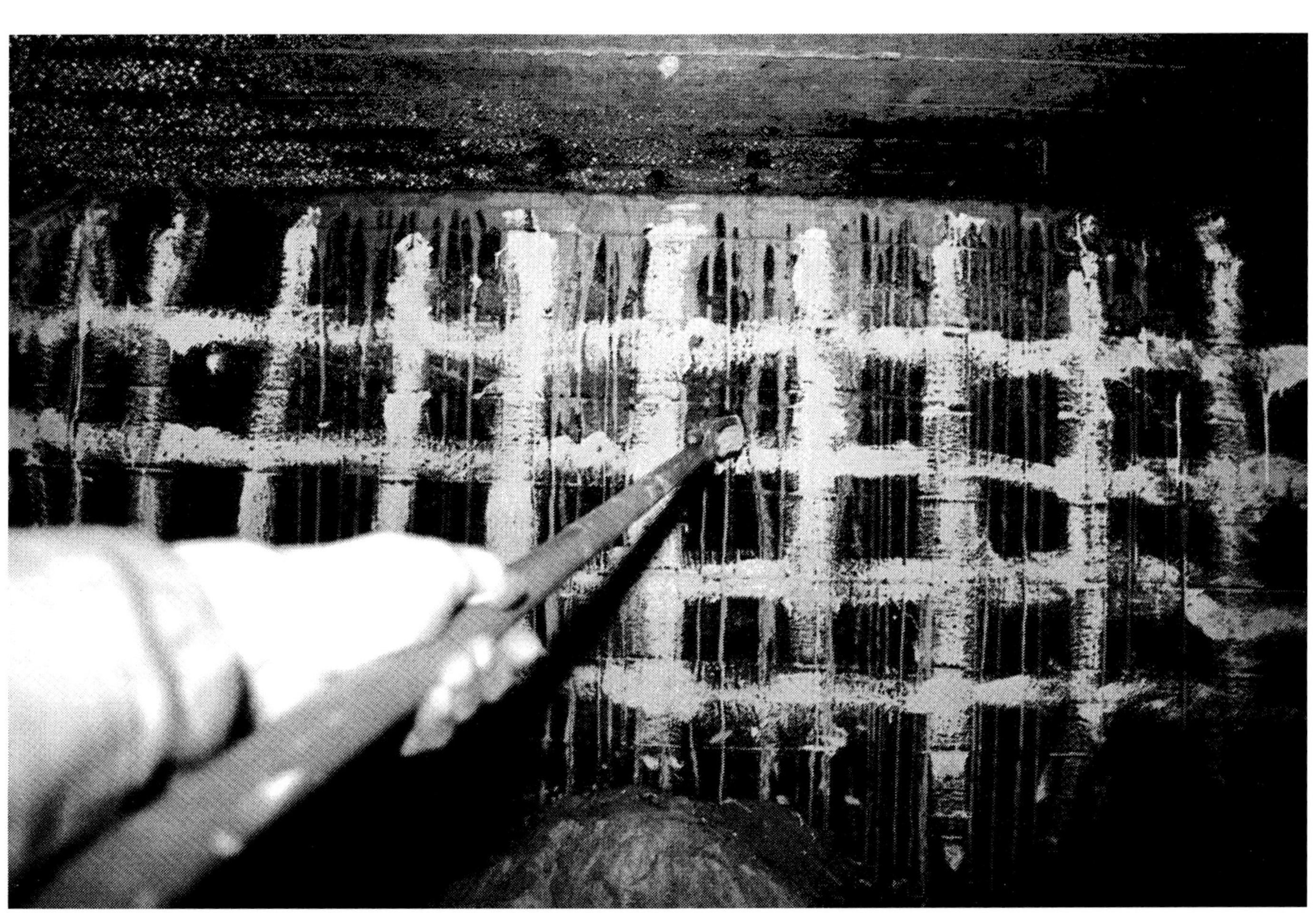

Interferences 1-7 (2004)
Antwerp (BE)

Interference 1 (2004)
Intervention at the former Military Hospital, Lange Leemstraat, Antwerp (BE)

Interference 2 (2004)
Intervention at the former Military Hospital, Lange Leemstraat, Antwerp (BE)

Interference 3 (2004)
Intervention at the former Military Hospital, Lange Leemstraat, Antwerp (BE)

Interference 4 (2004)
Intervention at the former Military Hospital, Lange Leemstraat, Antwerp (BE)

Interference 5: Rewiring (2004)
Intervention at Ledeganckkaai, Antwerp (BE)

Interference 6: Gone/ Demolished (2004)
Intervention at Ledeganckkaai, Antwerp (BE)

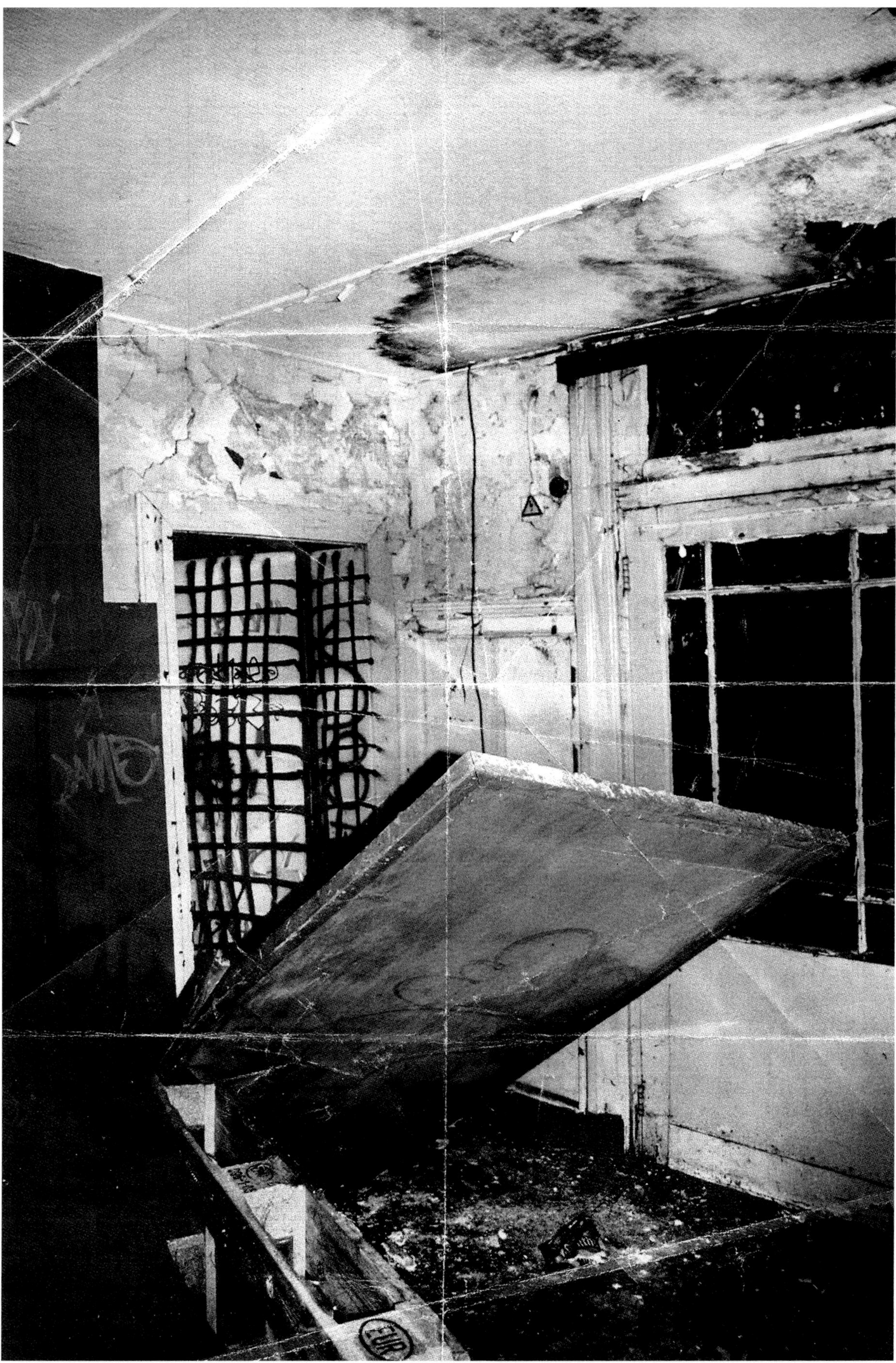
EUR

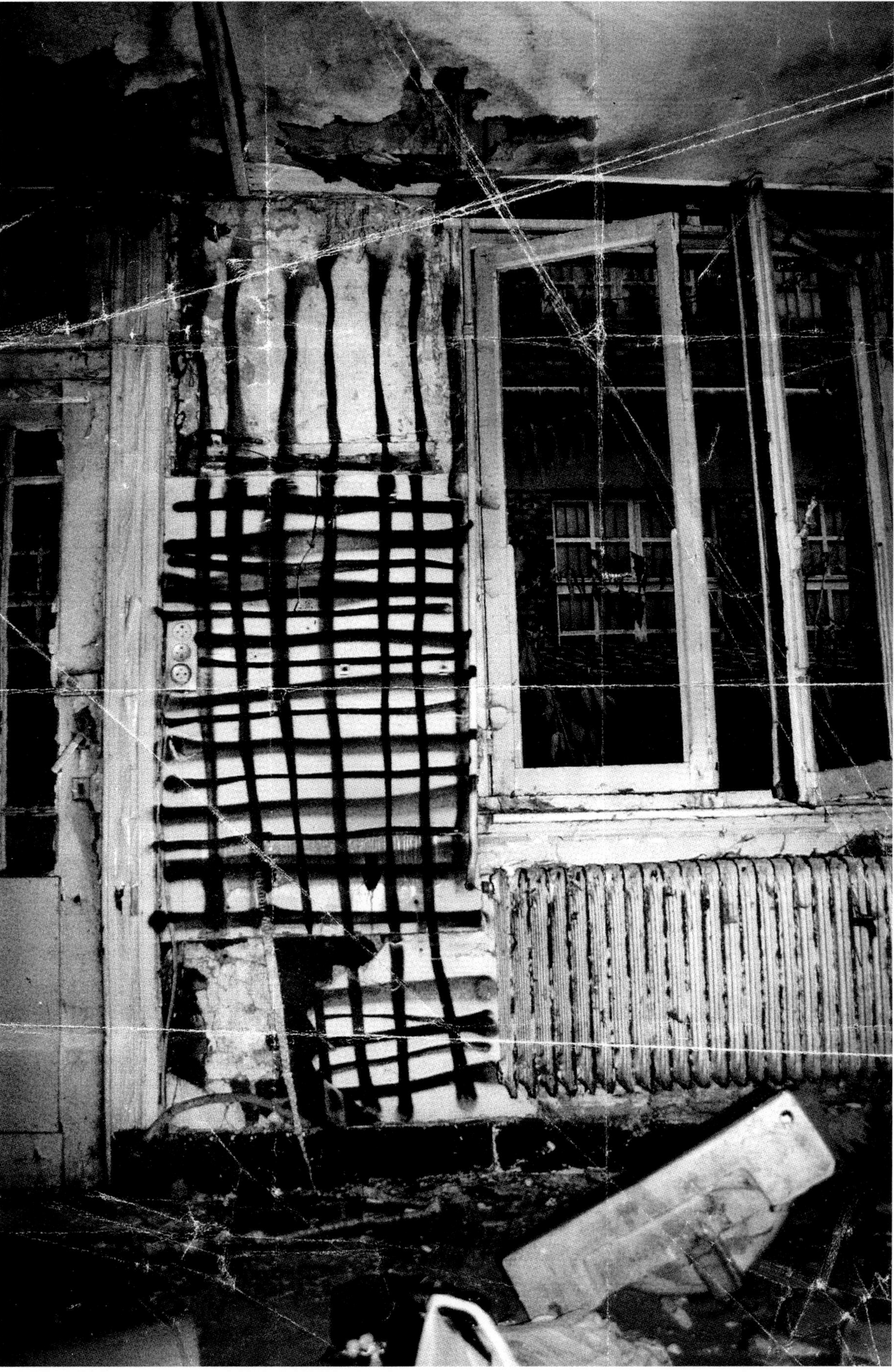

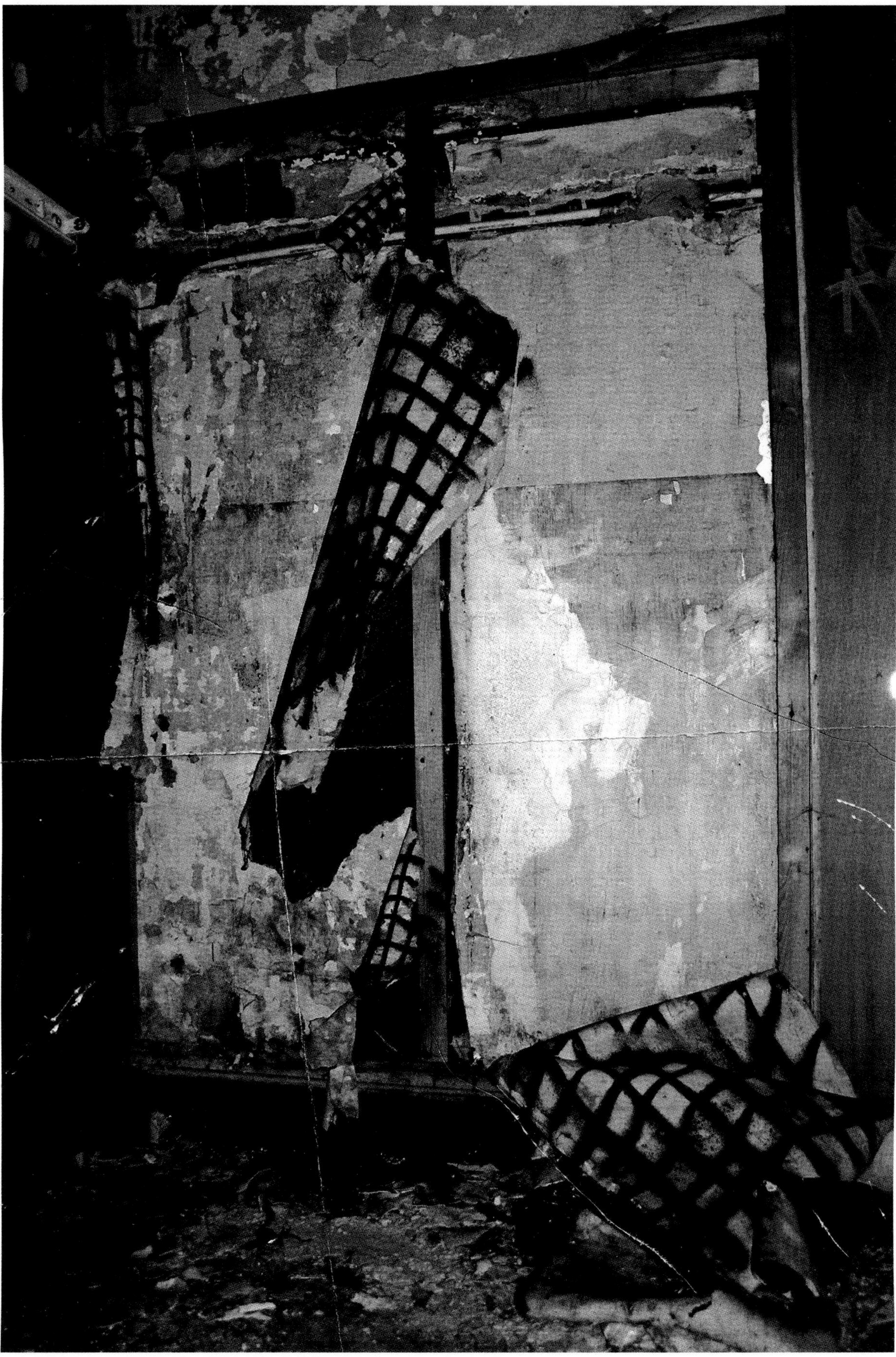

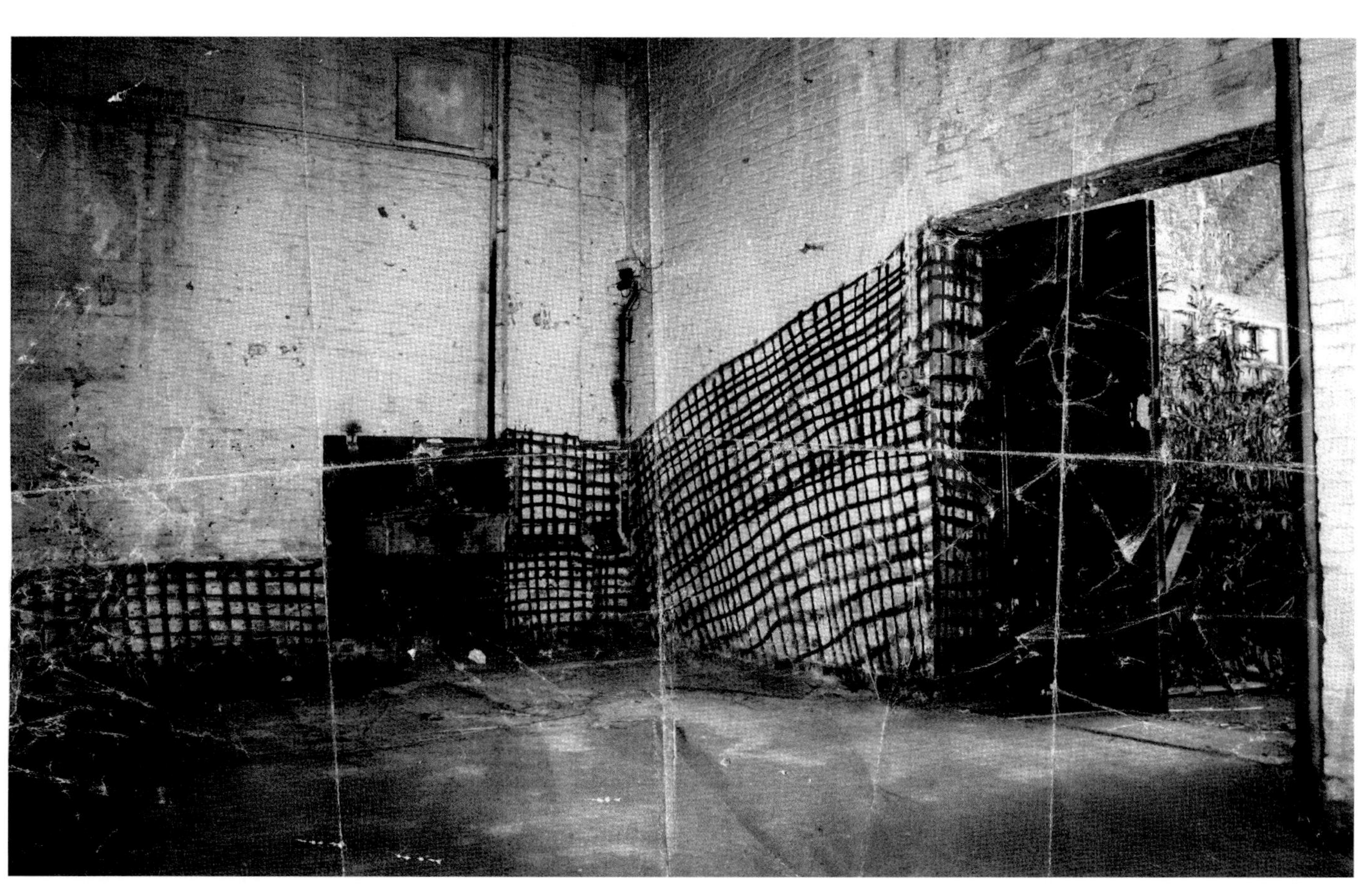

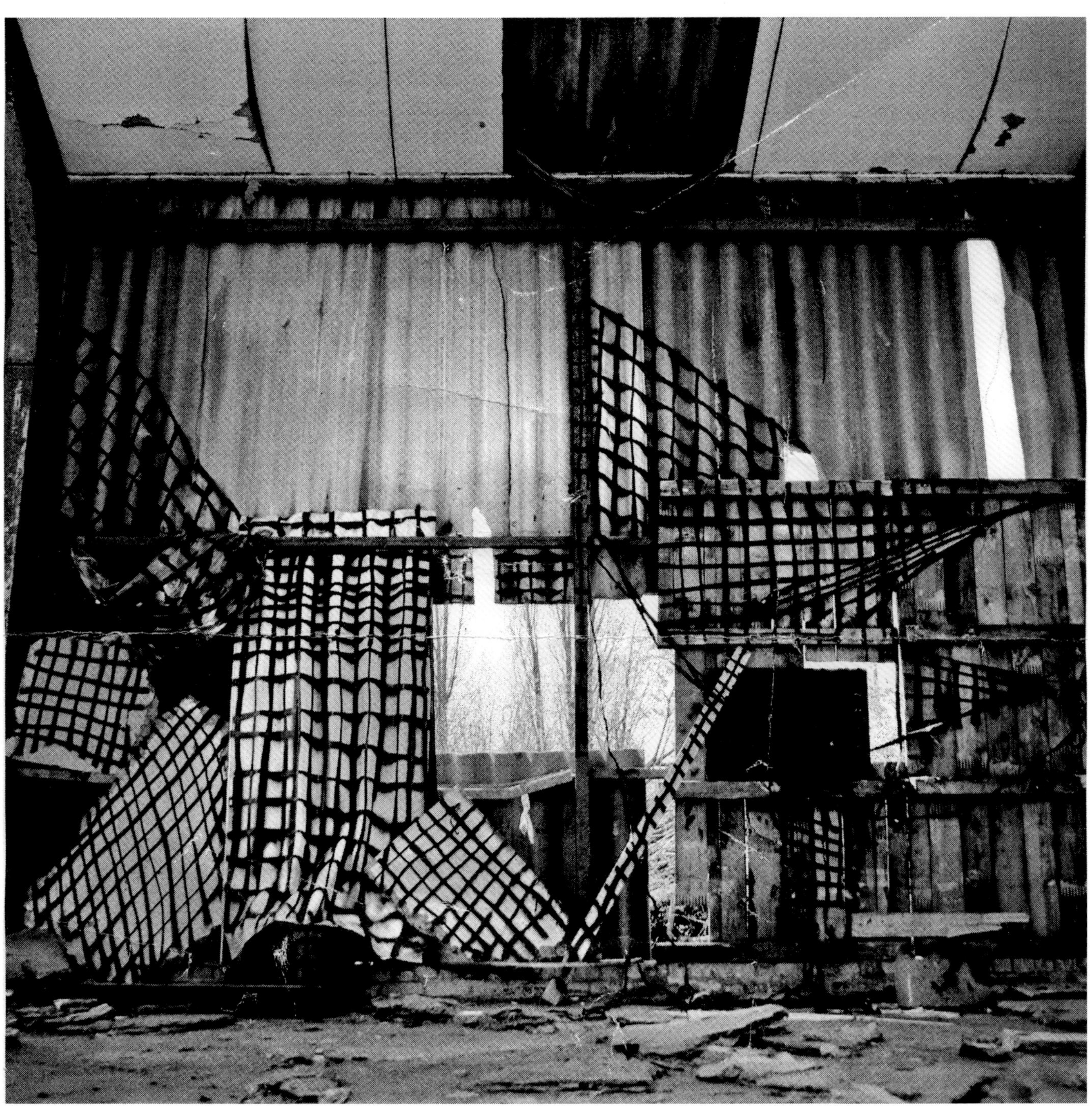

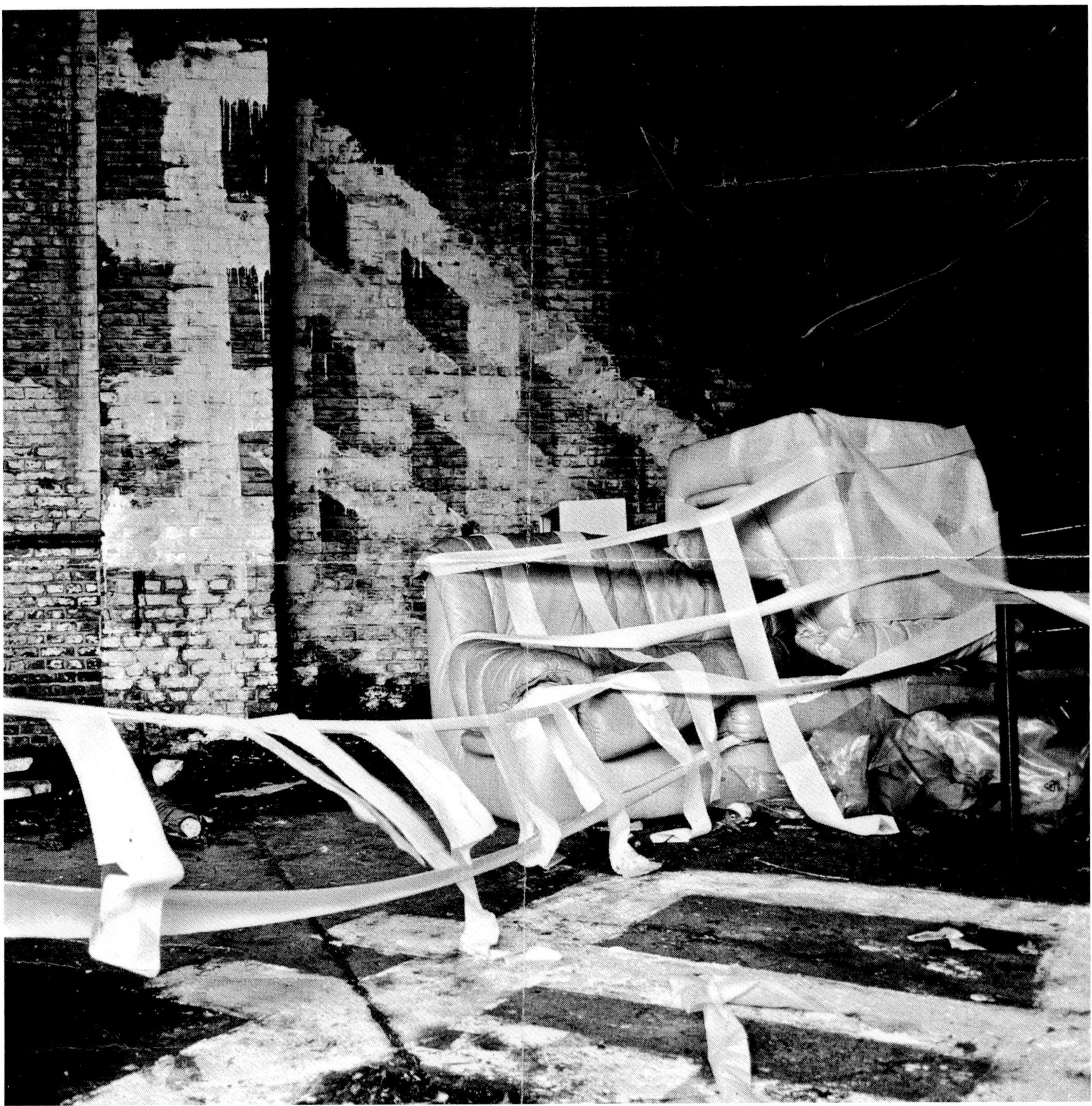

T.P.E.S. 1
invitation by word-of-mouth communication,
opened on 18.10.2005

T.P.E.S. 1 (2005)
Kerkstraat, Antwerp (BE)
abandoned house

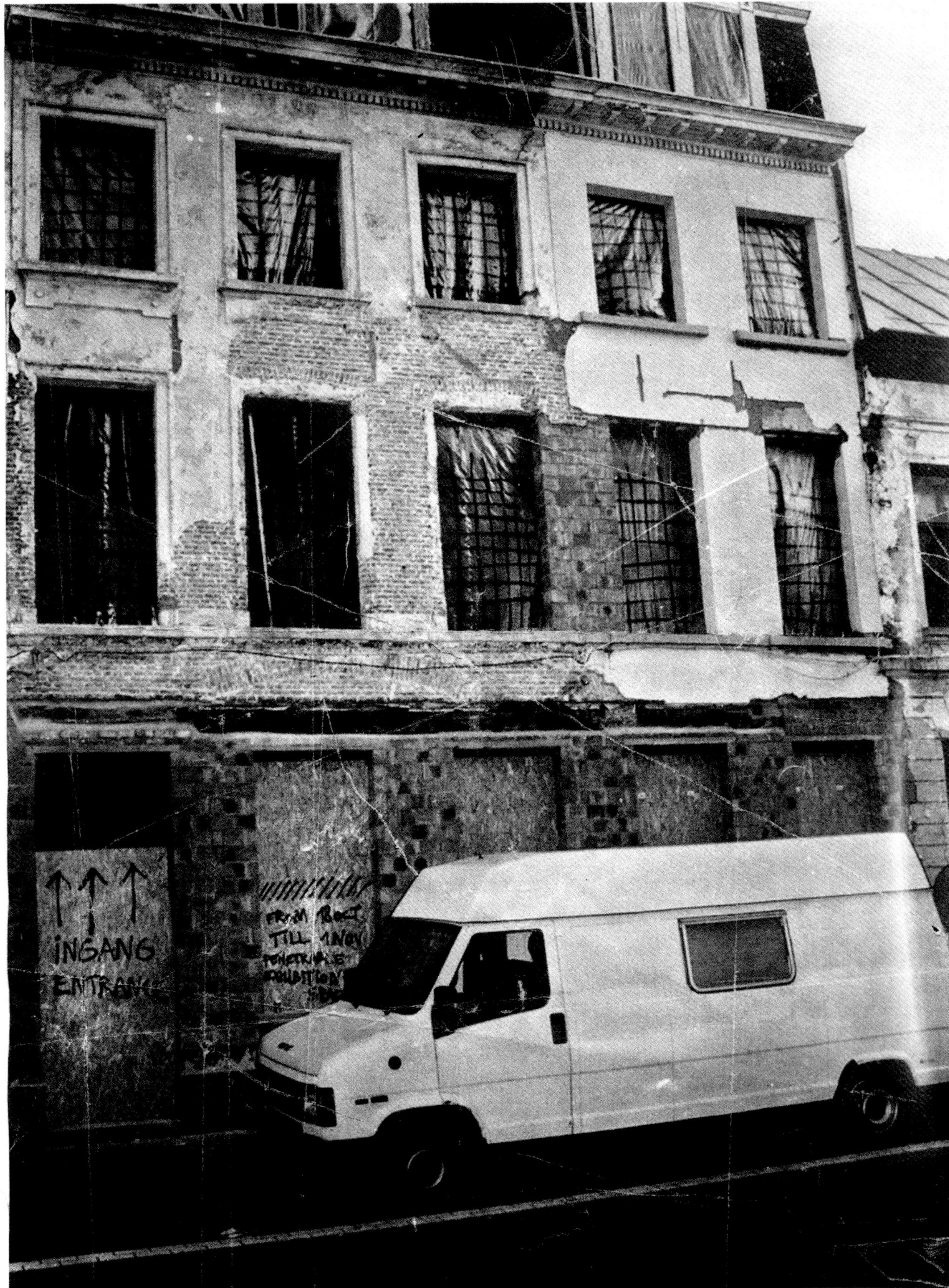
INGANG
ENTRANC
FROM
TILL 1 NOV

T.P.E.S. 2
invitation by an e-flyer,
opened on 25.11.2005

T.P.E.S. 2 (2005)
Begijnenstraat, Mechelen (BE)
abandoned house

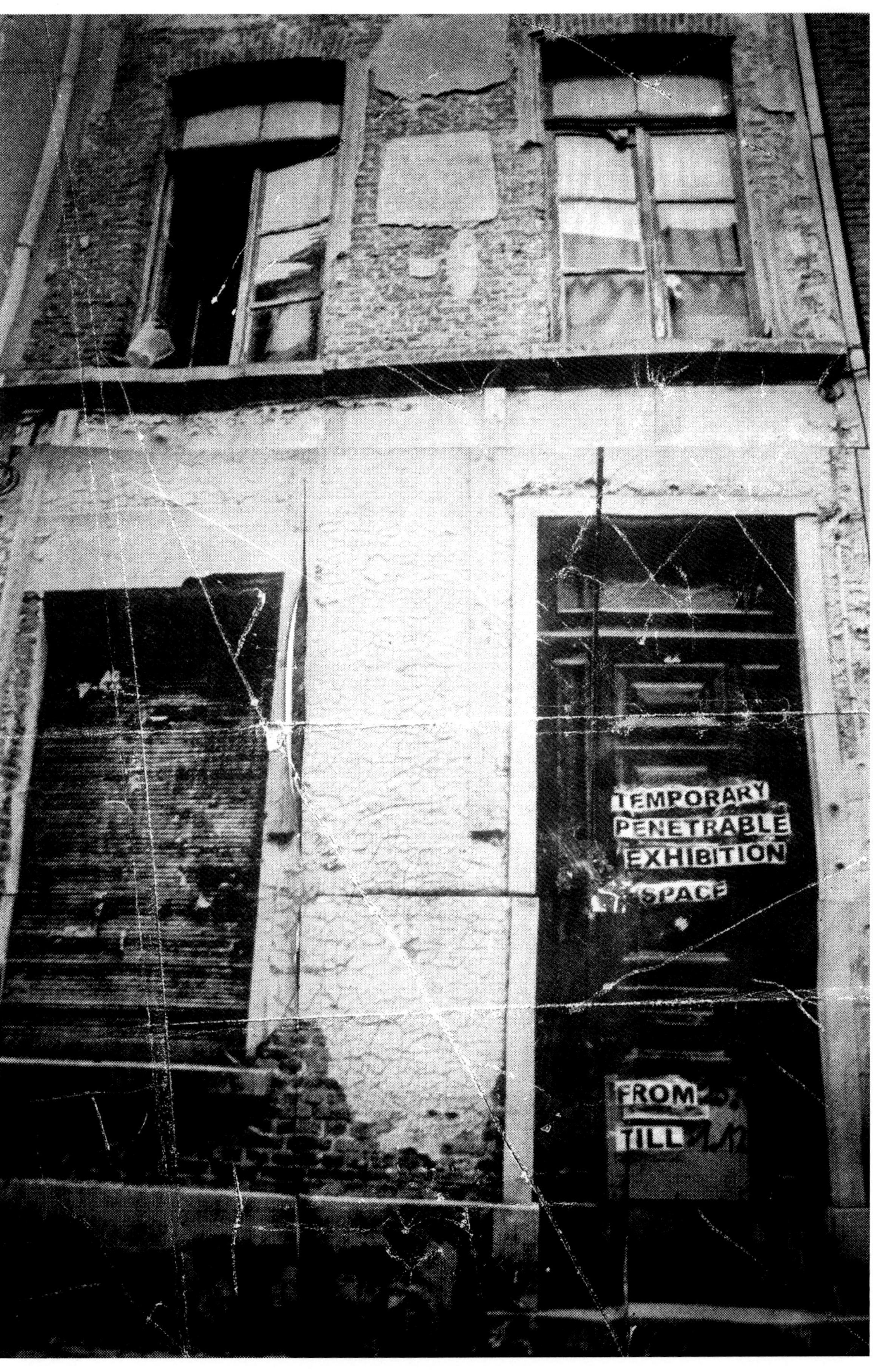
TEMPORARY
PENETRABLE
EXHIBITION
SPACE
FROM
TILL

T.P.E.S. 3
invitation through 'Base A'
an installation at artist-run
space Factor 44,
Bleekhofstraat,
Borgerhout (BE)
opened on 26.4.2006

T.P.E.S. 3 (1) (2006)
Plantin en Moretuslei 97,
Borgerhout (BE)
abandoned house

T.P.E.S. 3 (2) (2006)
Wipstraat 37,
Borgerhout (BE)
(no image)
abandoned house

T.P.E.S. 3 (3) (2006)
Van Immerseelstraat,
Borgerhout (BE)
abandoned railway building

T.P.E.S. 3 (4) (2006)
Lange Kievitstraat 88,
Borgerhout (BE)
abandoned house

T.P.E.S. 3 (5) (2006)
Ploegstraat,
Borgerhout (BE)
spaypainted wall

T.P.E.S. 3 (6) (2006)
Ploegstraat - Provinciestraat,
Borgerhout (BE)
empty lot

T.P.E.S. 3 (7) (2006)
Provinciestraat,
Borgerhout (BE)
abandoned house

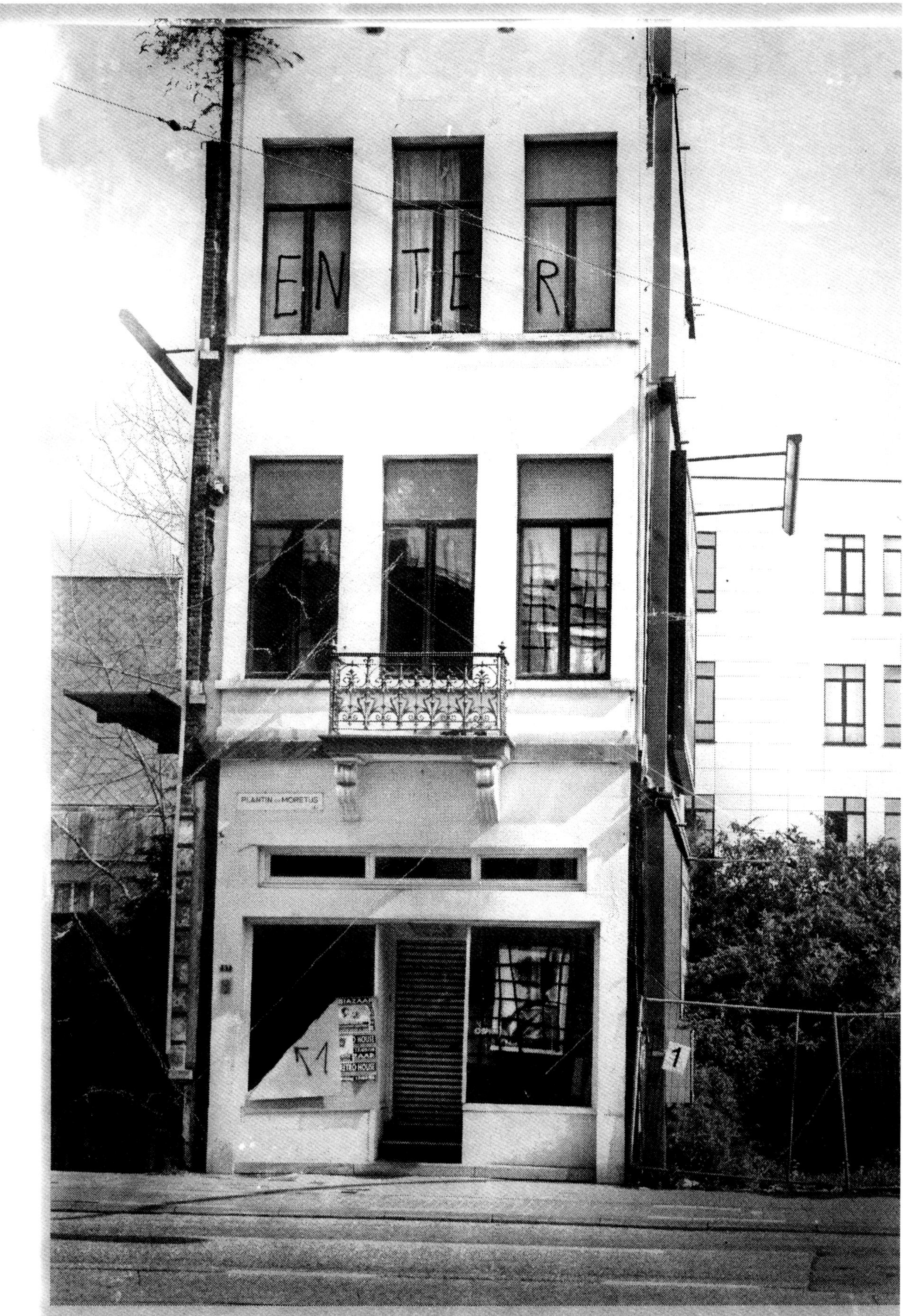
ENTER
PLANTIN MORETUS
1

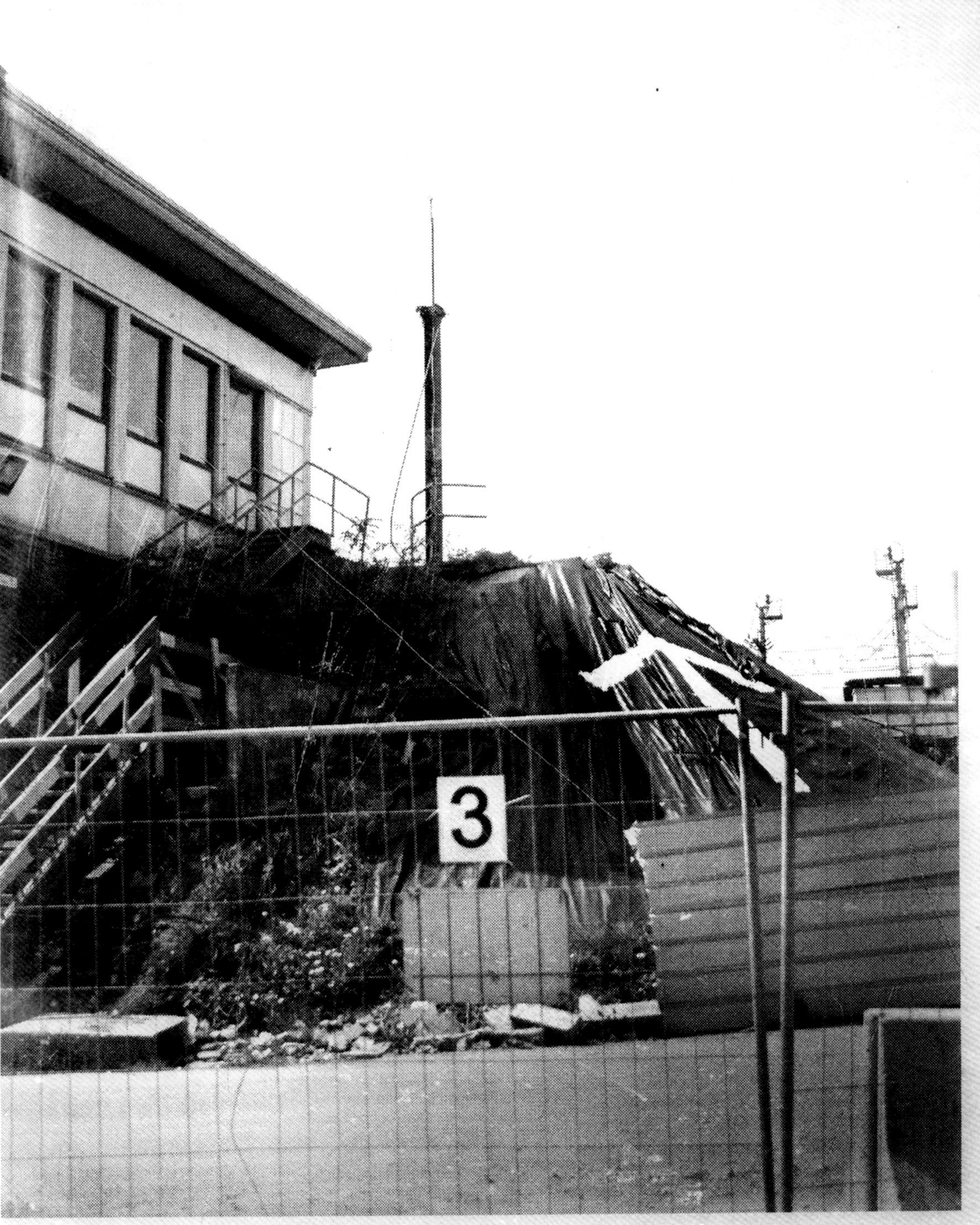
3

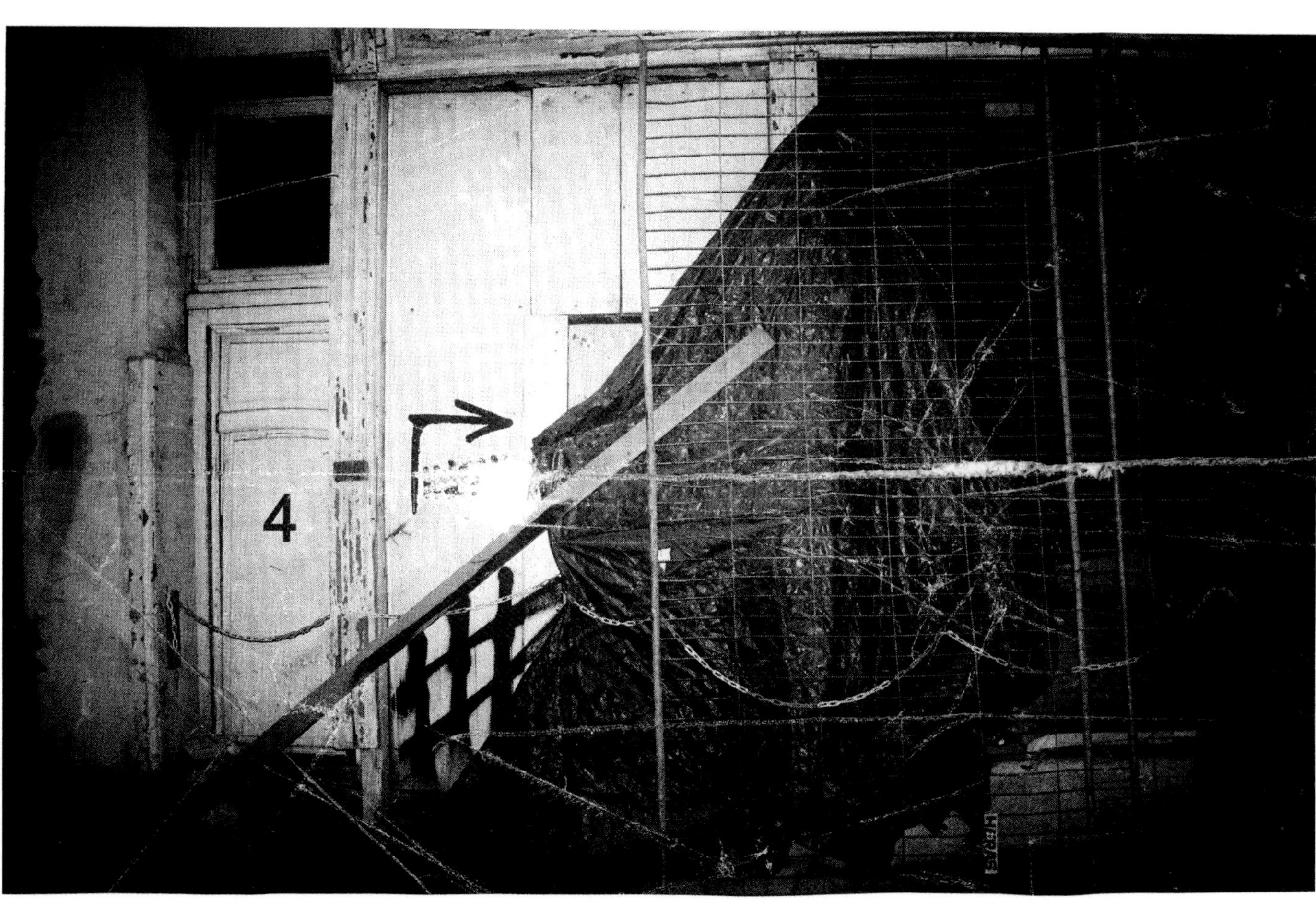
4

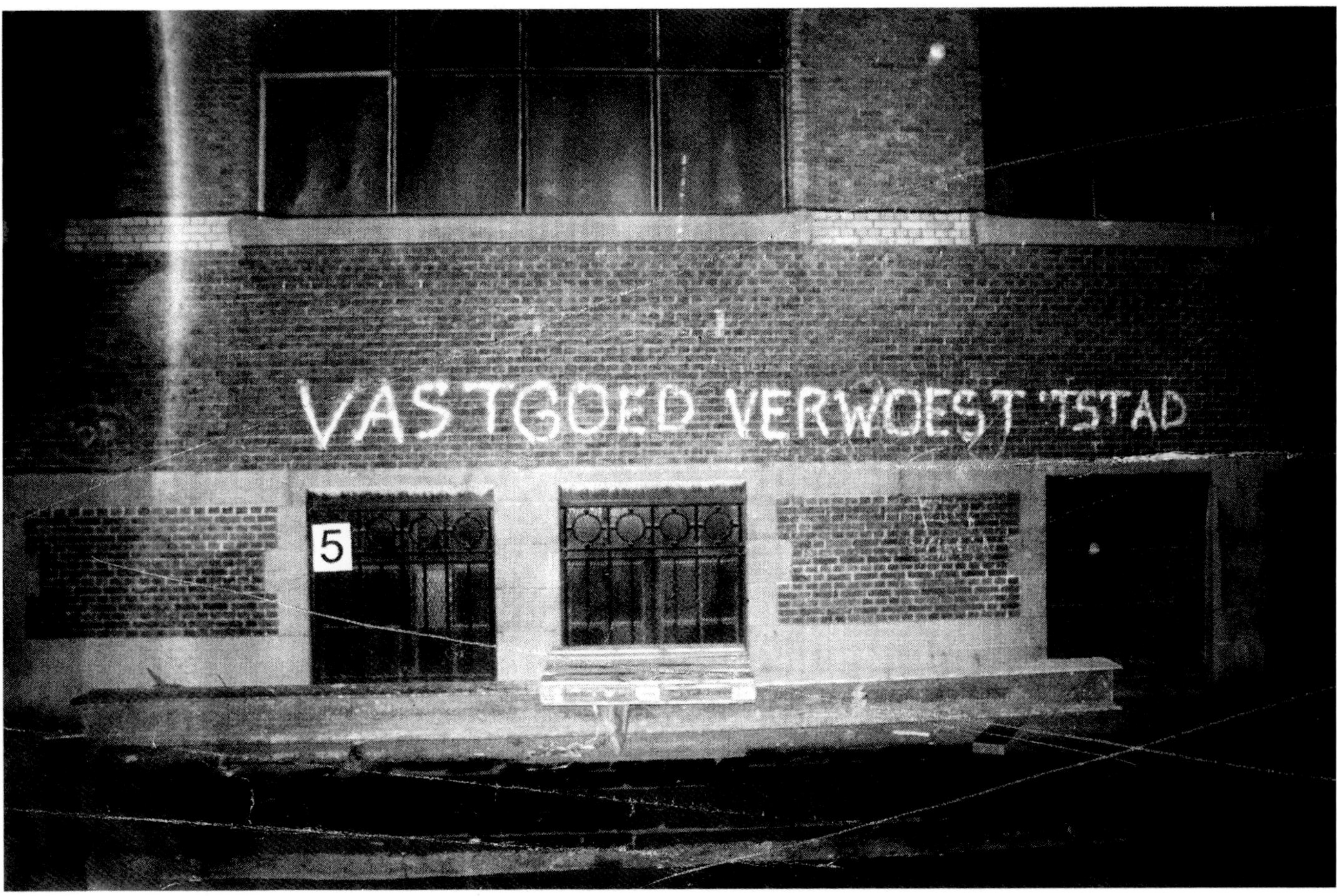
VASTGOED VERWOEST 'T STAD
5

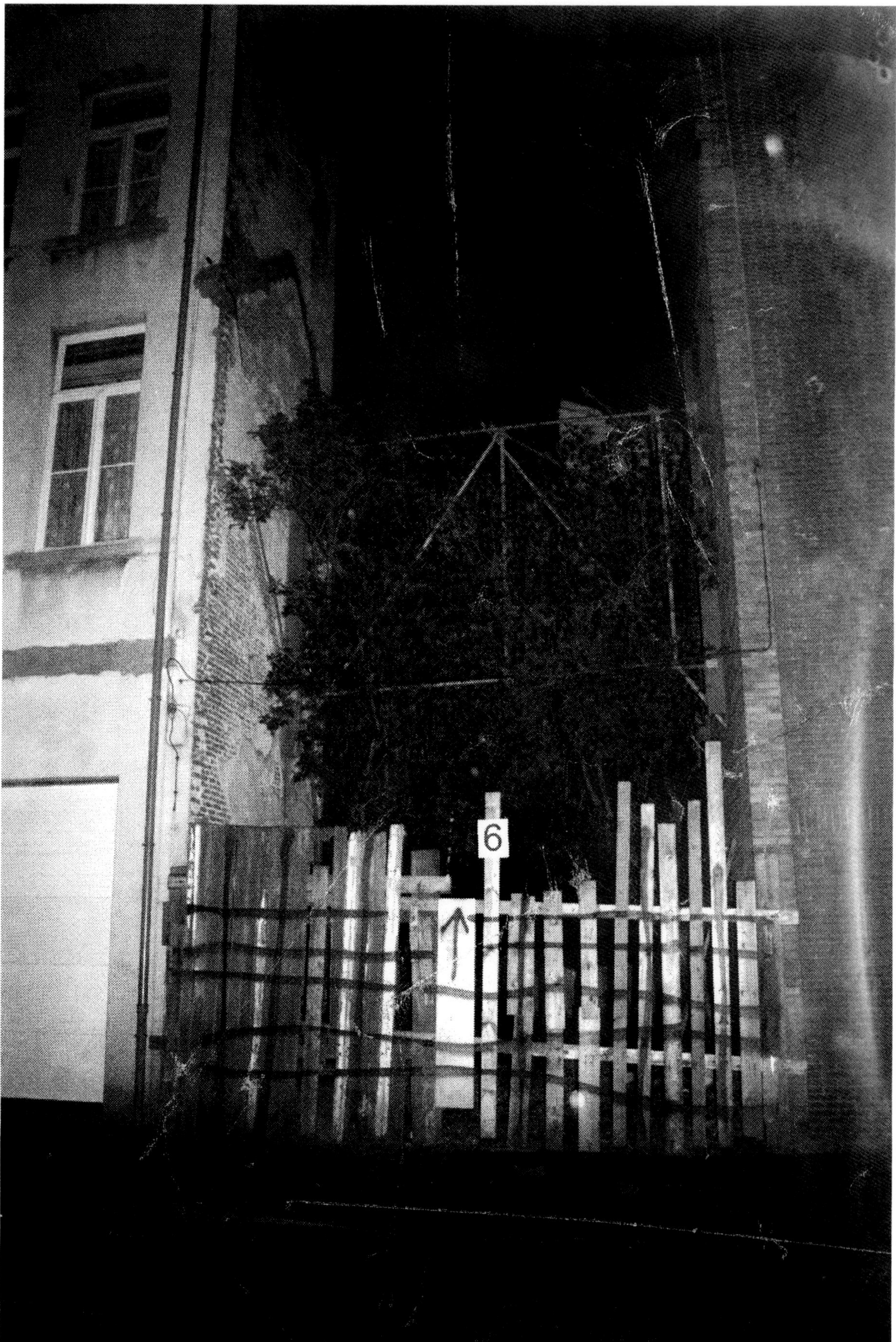
6

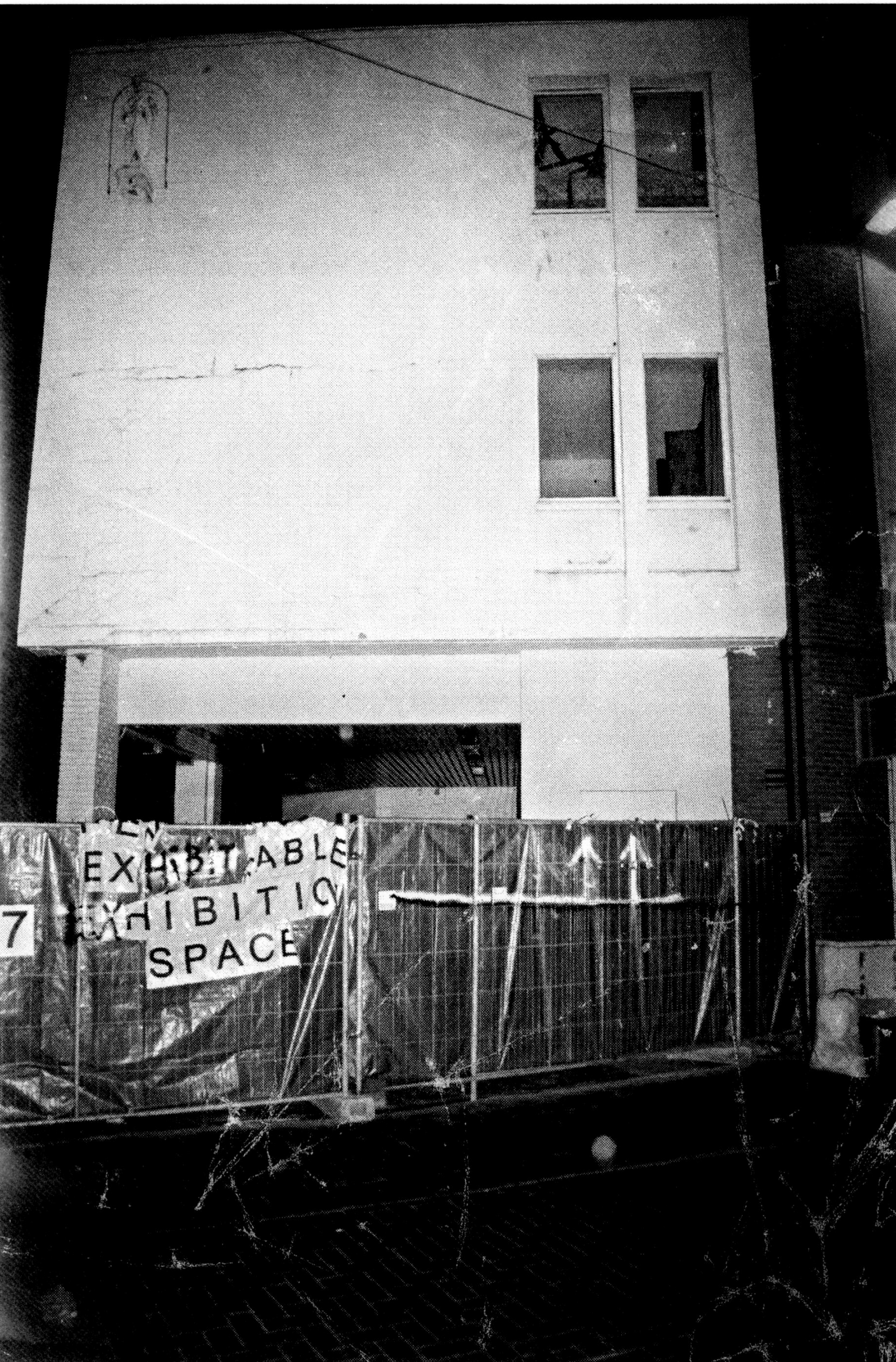
SPACE

T.P.E.S. 4
invitation through a soloshow
at Gallery Wilfried Lentz,
Rotterdam (NL)
opened on 9.10.2008

T.P.E.S. 4 (2008)
Schiestraat,
Rotterdam (NL)
abandoned sculpture
by J.H. Baas which
was part of the former
Rotterdam Central
railway station

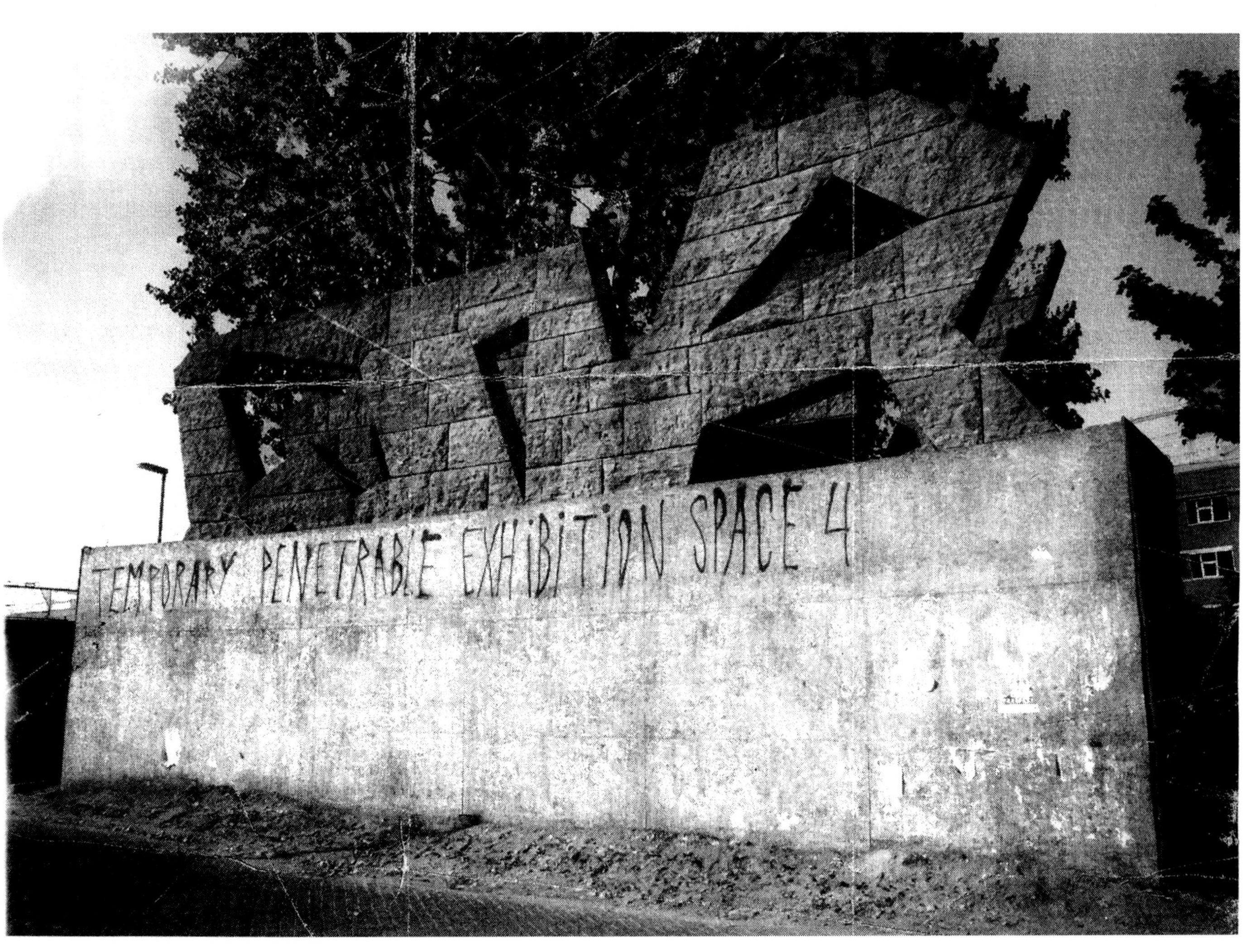
TEMPORARY PENETRABLE EXHIBITION SPACE 4

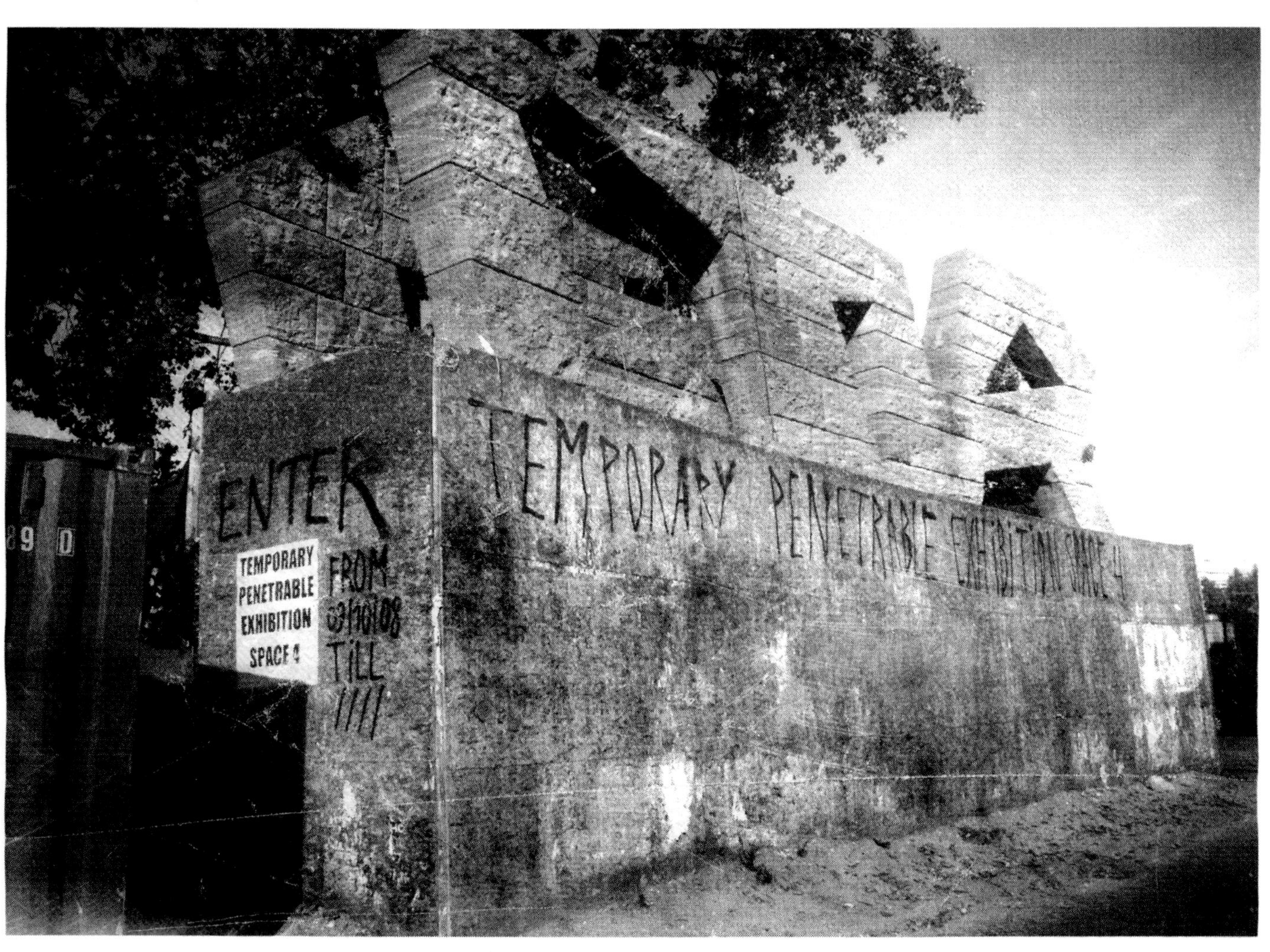
ENTER
TEMPORARY
PENETRABLE
EXHIBITION
SPACE 4
FROM
TILL
TEMPORARY PENETRABLE EXHIBITION SPACE 4

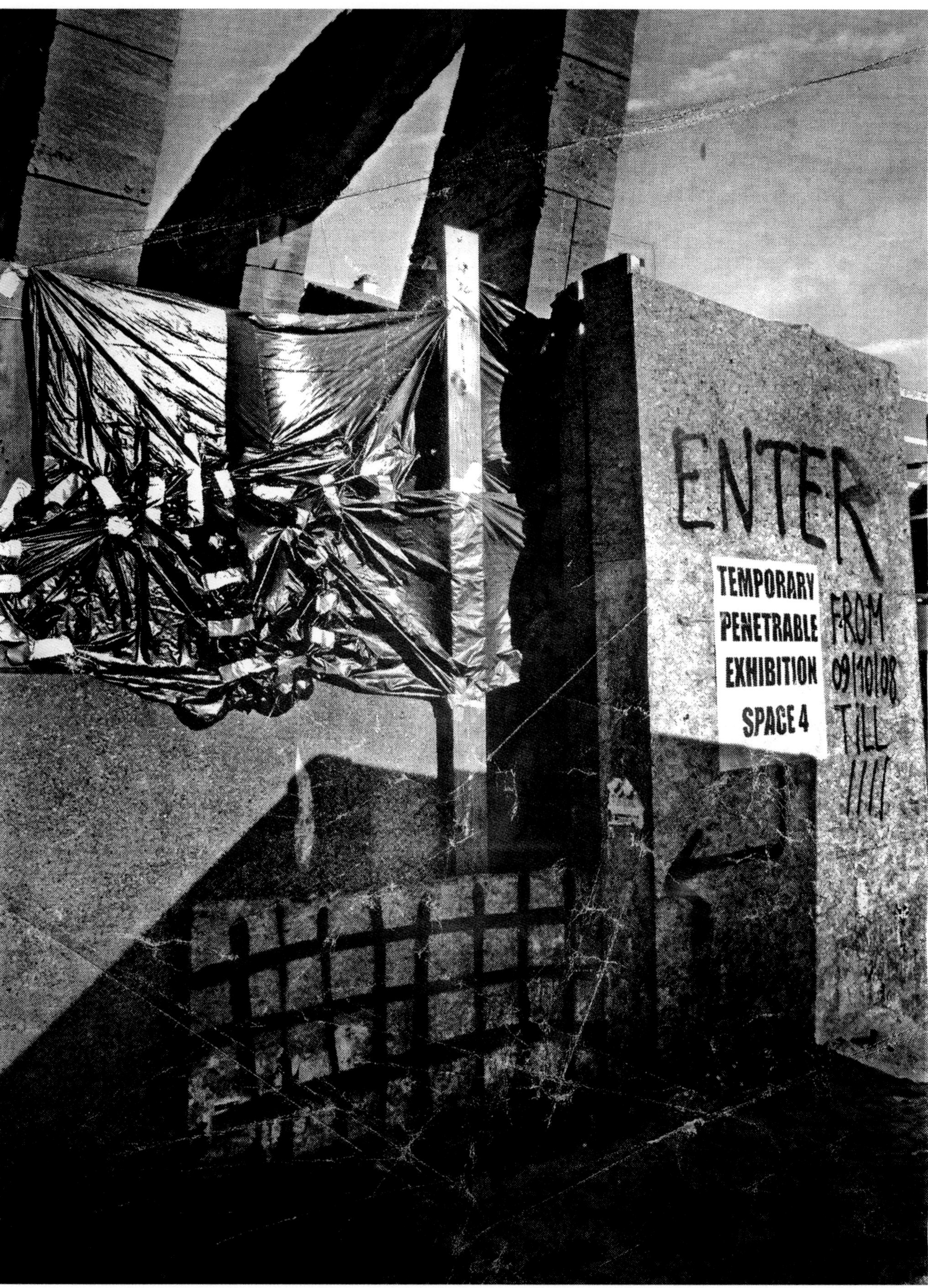
ENTER
TEMPORARY
PENETRABLE
EXHIBITION
SPACE 4
FROM
09/10/08
TILL

T.P.E.S. 5
invitation through a
private view at
Vienna International
Apartment,
Brussels (BE)
opened on 16.10.2009

T.P.E.S. 5,
Trapstraat,
Brussels (BE)
empty lot with
an entrance to a
former basement

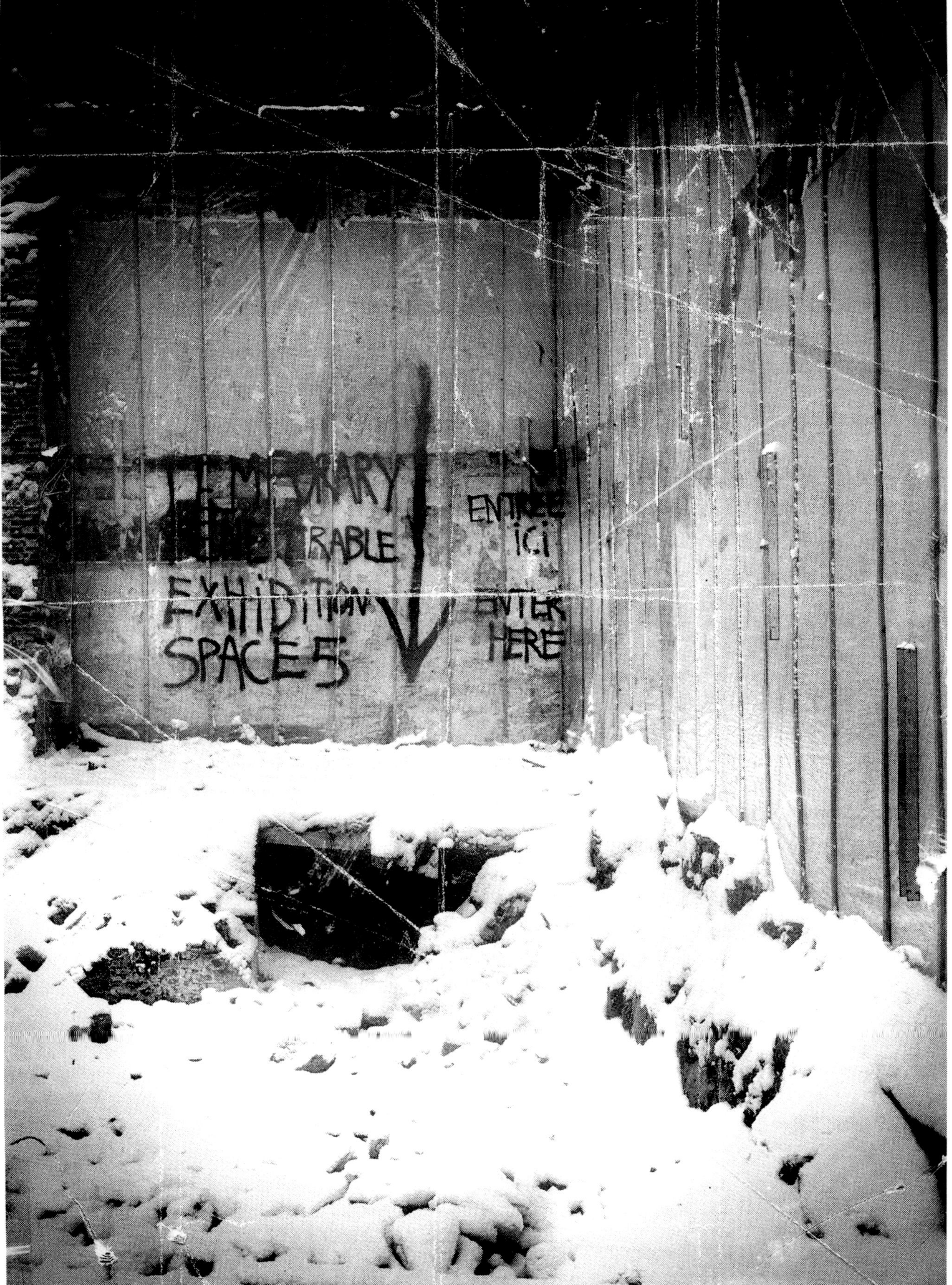
EXHIBITION
SPACE 5
ENTREE
ICI
ENTER
HERE

T.P.E.S. 6
invitation through an
art festival (Freestate II),
Oostende (BE)
opened on 25.6.2011

T.P.E.S. 6,
Slipwaykaai,
Oostende (BE)
abandoned building

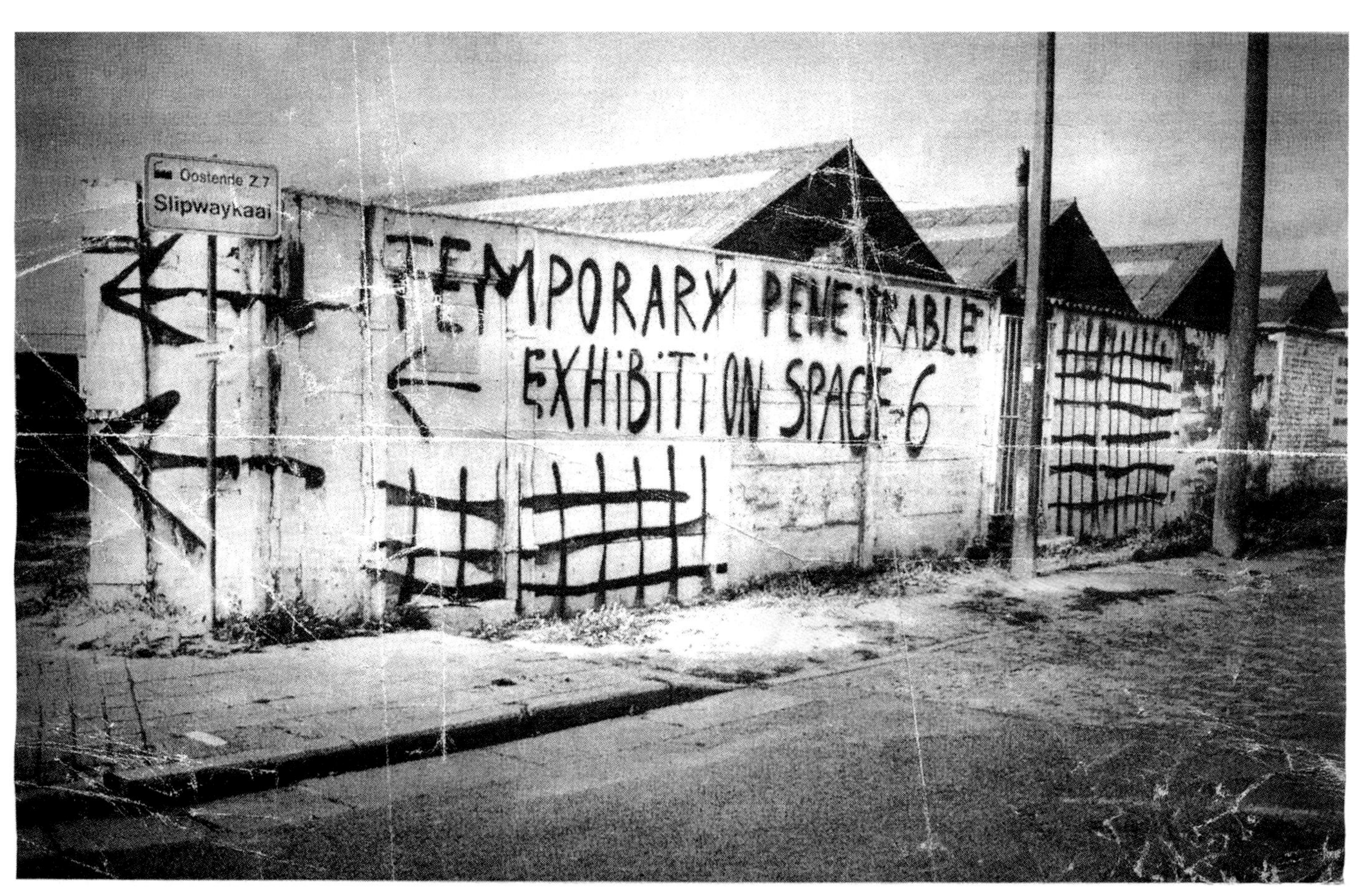
Oostende Z.7
Slipwaykaai
TEMPORARY PENETRABLE
EXHIBITION SPACE 6

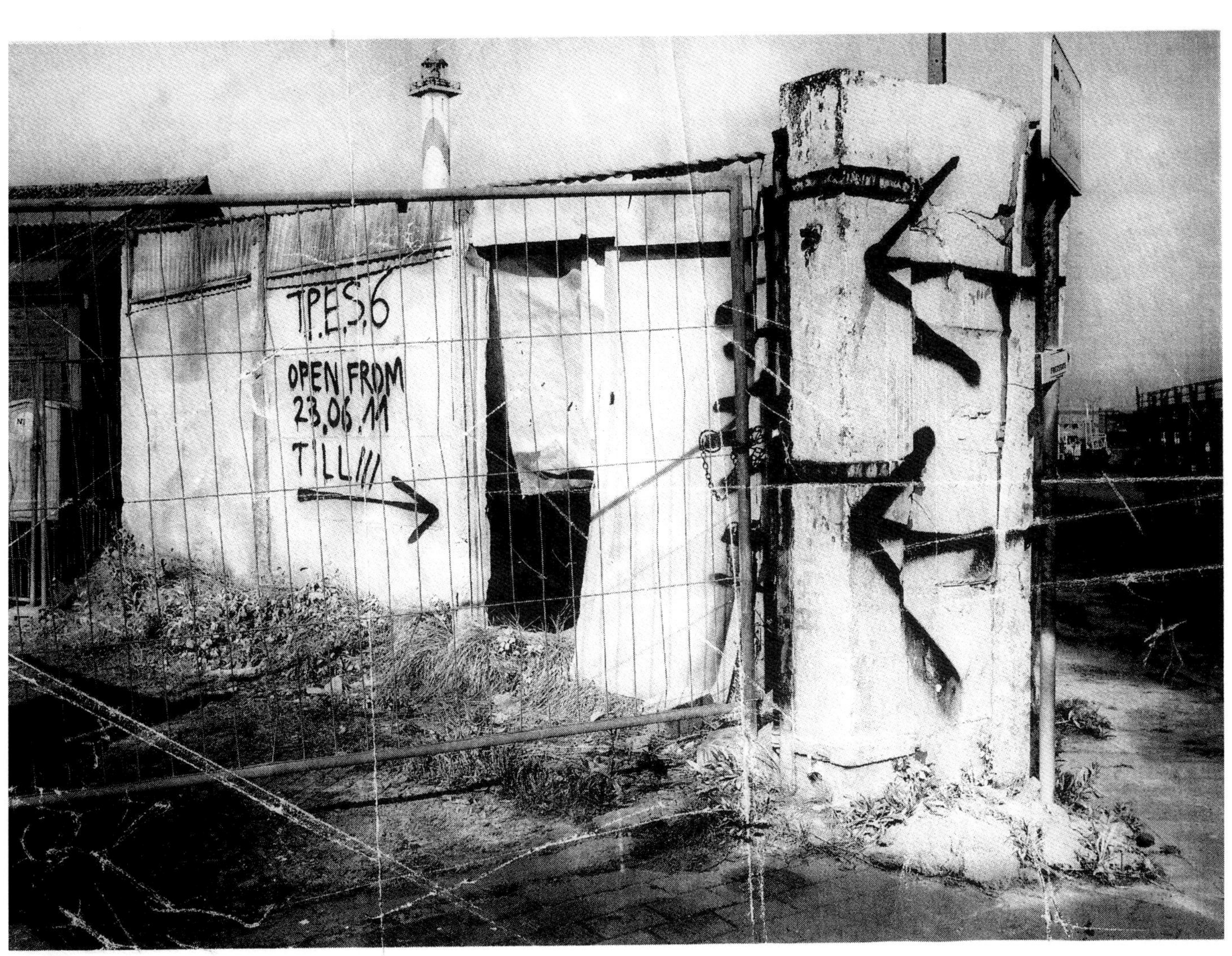
T.P.E.S.6
OPEN FROM
23.06.11
TILL!!!

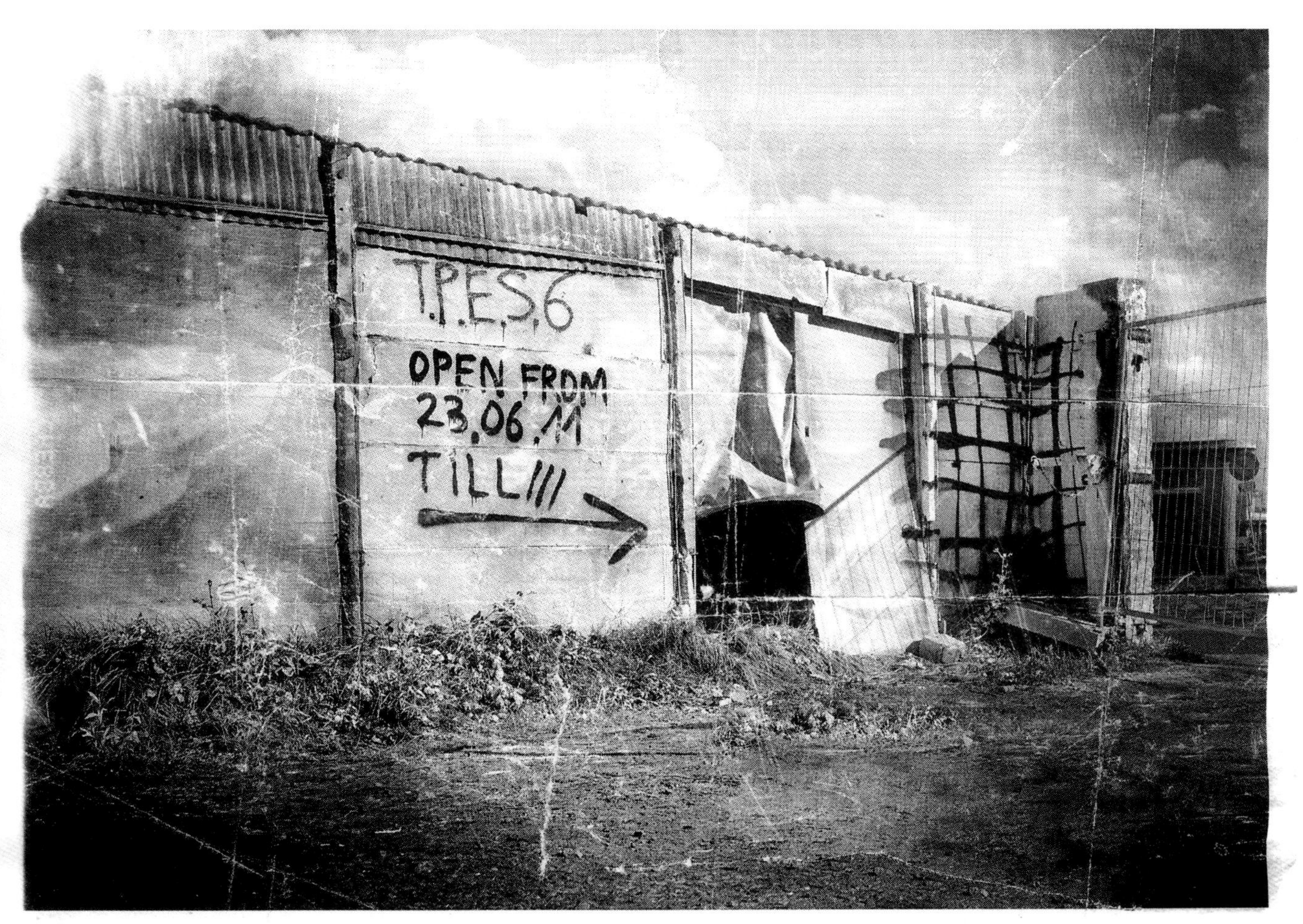
T.P.E.S.6
OPEN FROM
23.06.11
TILL///

T.P.E.S. 7(1)
invited through an
open studio event
at the Rijksakademie,
Amsterdam (NL)
opened on 1.12.2012

T.P.E.S. 7 (1)
documentation of
intervention at atelier
during open studios

former unreachable
part of the Rijksakademies
building complex

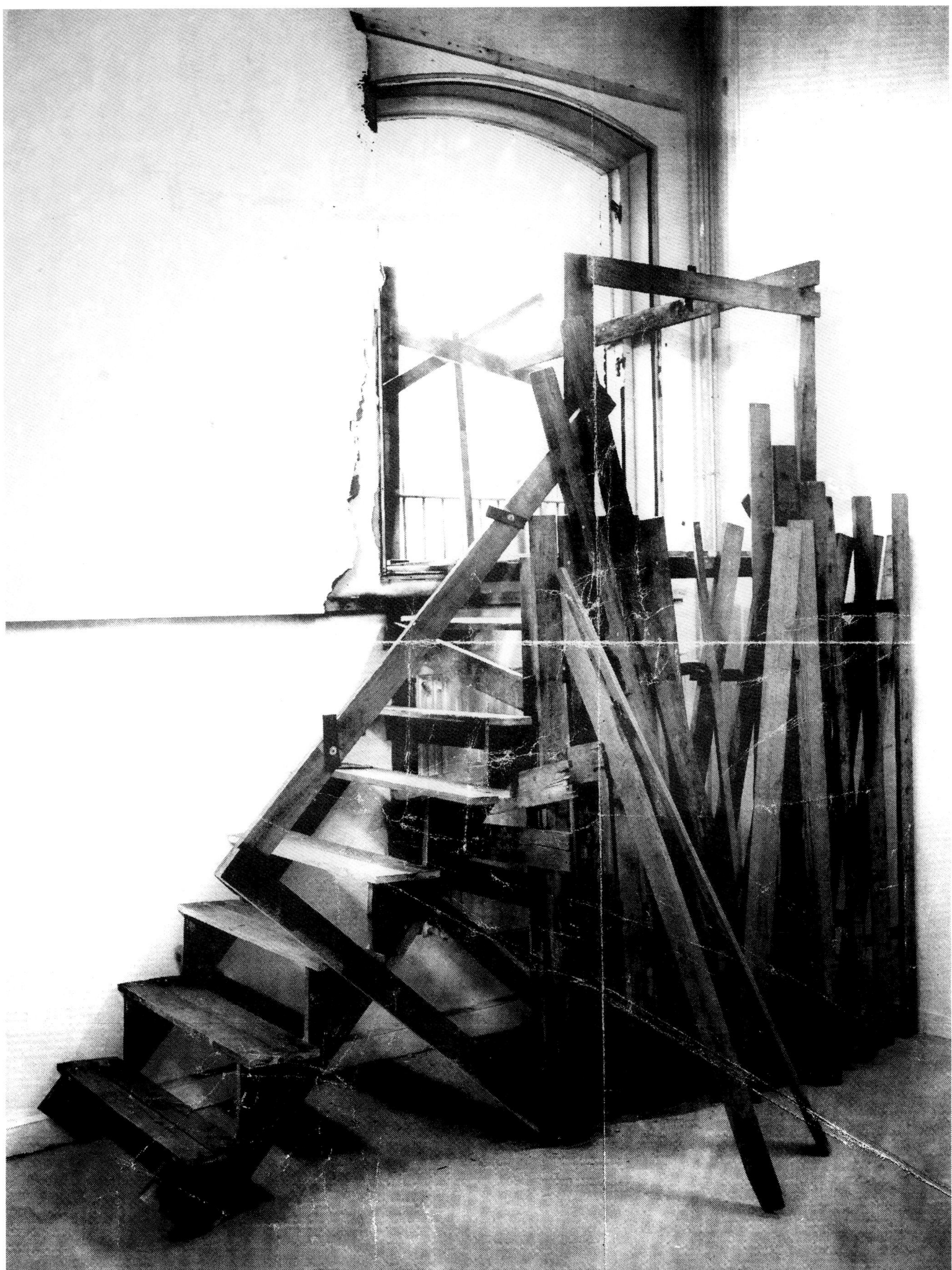

T.P.E.S.7 (2)
invited through a lecture
at 'Translation Acts -
The world is Not Fair'
for Raumexperimente,
Berlin (D)
opened on 7.6.2012

photographs of lecture
and announcement
of T.P.E.S. 7 (2)
no images of the actual T.P.E.S.

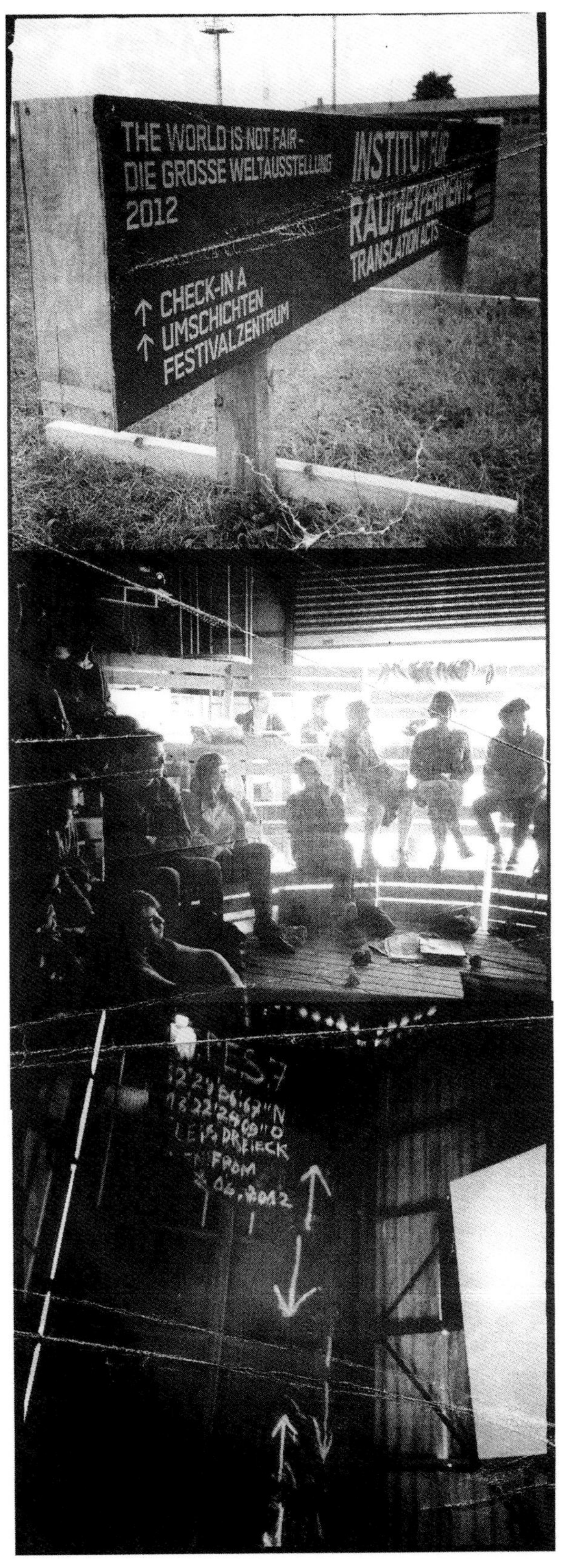
THE WORLD IS NOT FAIR -
DIE GROSSE WELTAUSSTELLUNG
2012
INSTITUT FÜR
RAUMEXPERIMENTE
TRANSLATION ACTS
↑ CHECK-IN A
UMSCHICHTEN
↑ FESTIVALZENTRUM

T.P.E.S.7 (3)
invited through a scene in
a video work, part of the
installation "Looking Back
While Walking Forward"
at Bozar, Brussels (BE)
opened on 7.5.2013

T.P.E.S.7 (3)
tunnel below an abandoned
cooling tower
Charleroi (BE)

entrance of T.P.E.S. 7(3)
as it appears in the
videowork Looking Back
While Walking Forward

documentation of
entering T.P.E.S. 7(3)

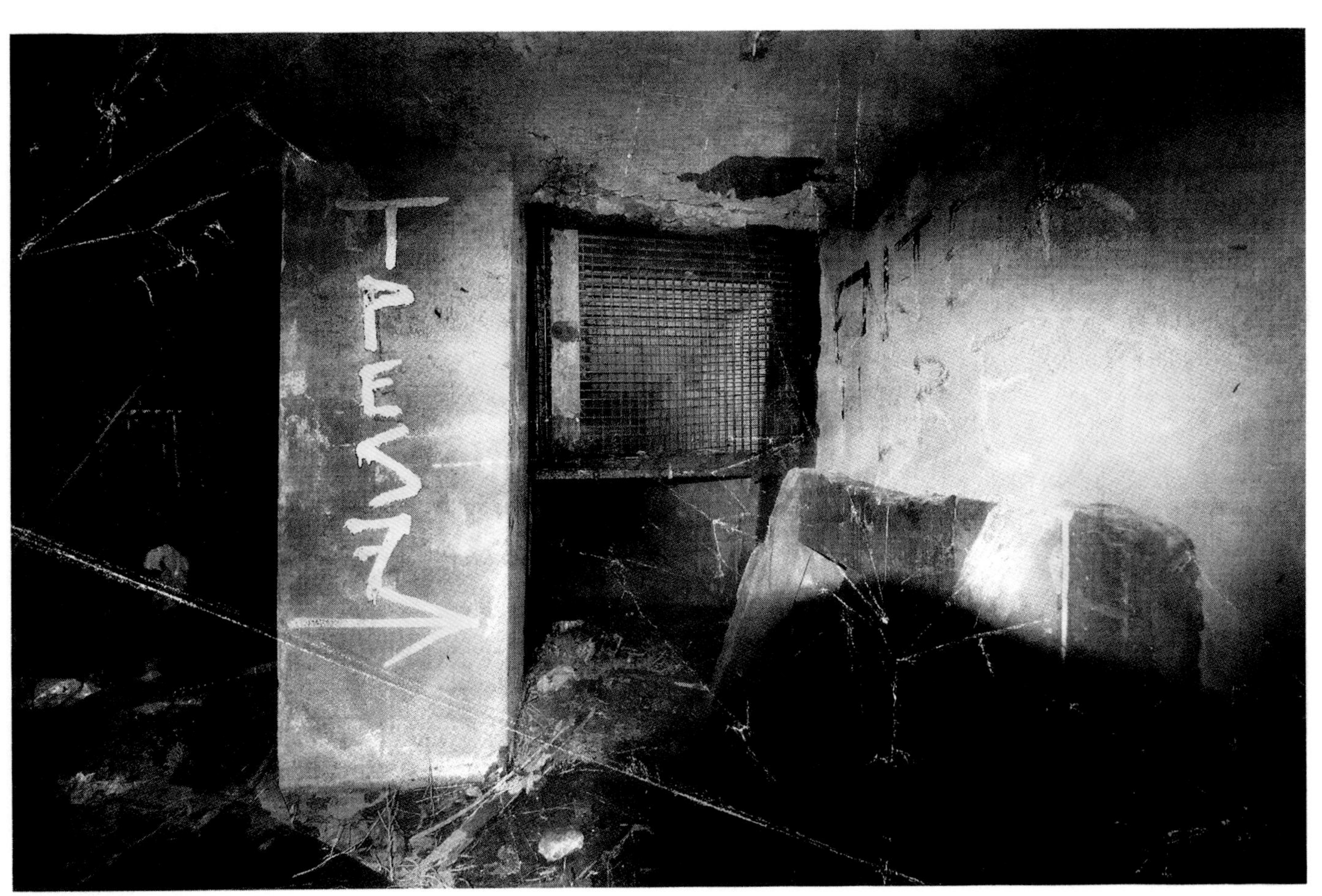
TPESZ

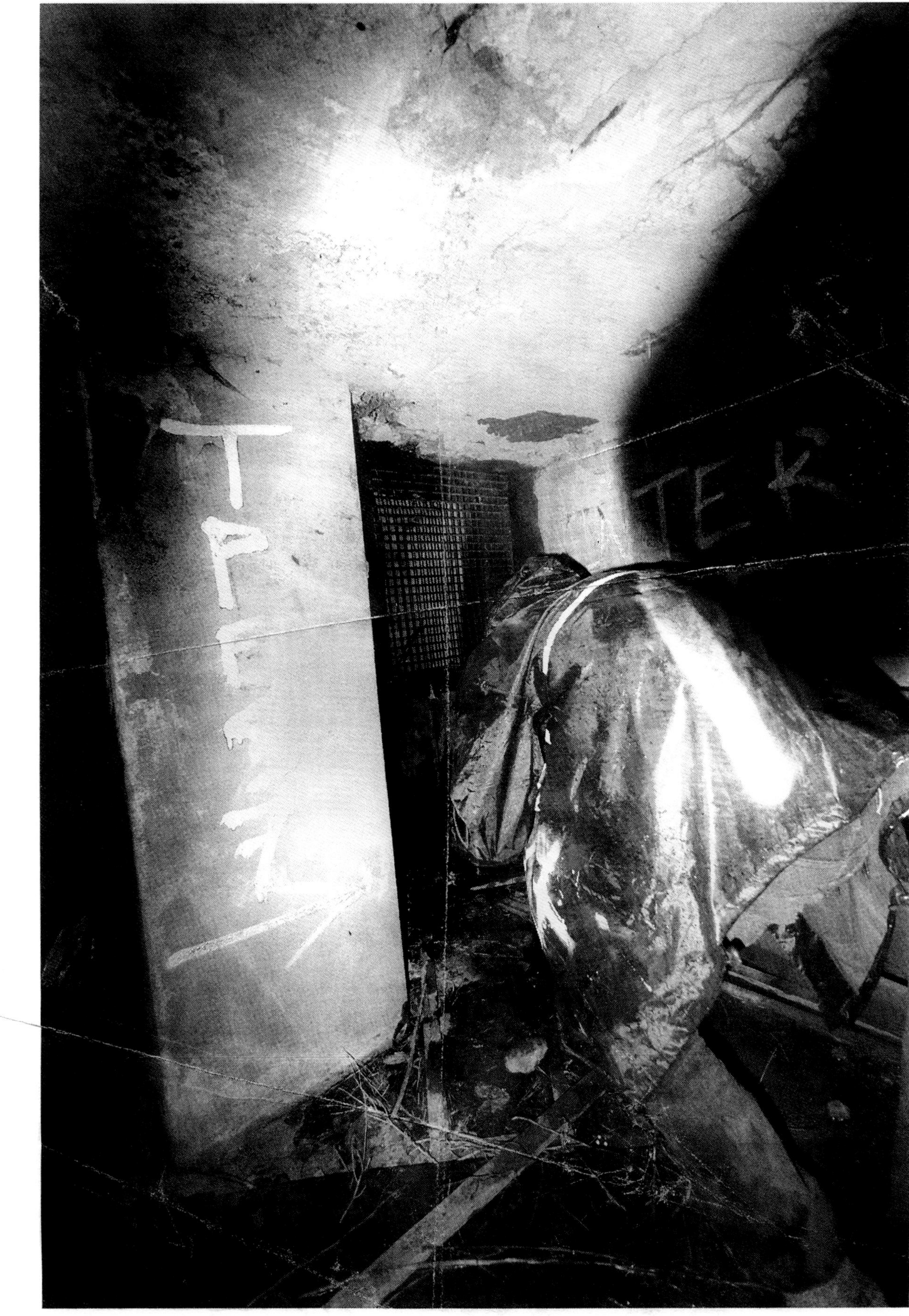

T.P.E.S. 8
invited through an exhibition,
part of an exchange
programme between NICC
and Espace 251 Nord,
at Extra City, Antwerp (BE)
and Ravi Liège (BE)
opened on 21.3.2014

T.P.E.S. 8
Impasse Macors,
Liège (BE)
entrance to a
ruin structure

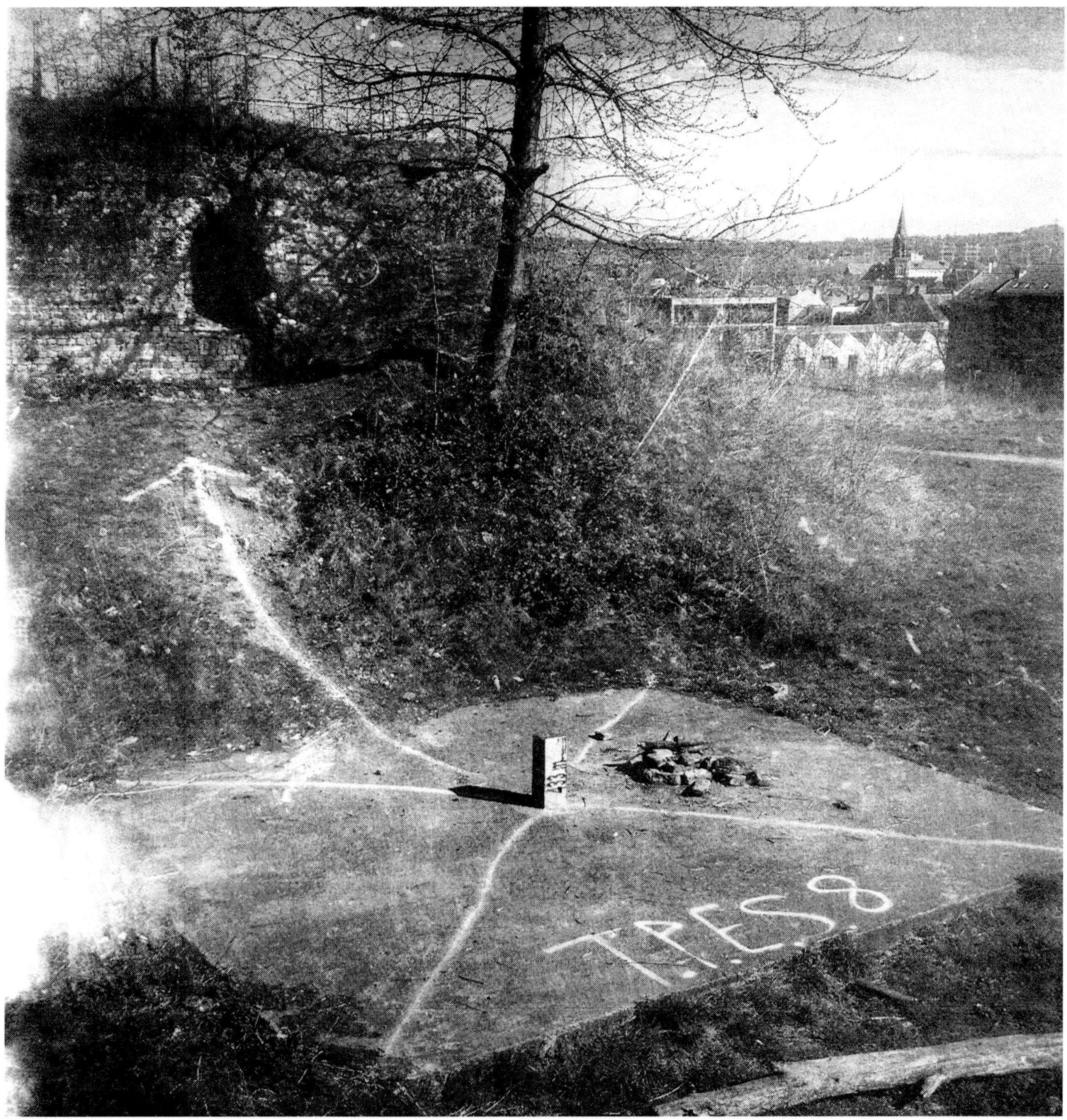
T.P.E.S. 8

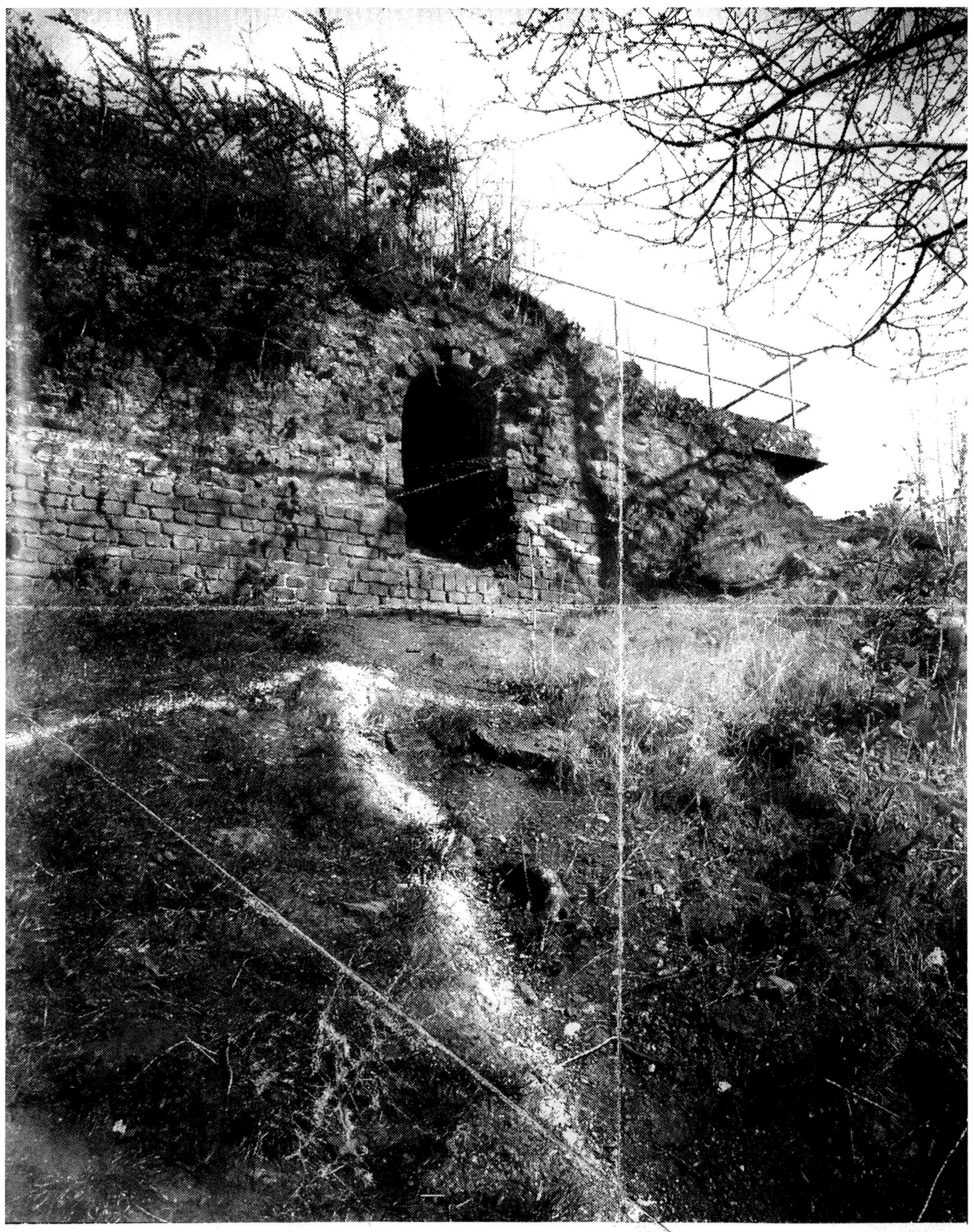

no invitations were made for this series of Temporary Penetrable Exhibition Spaces. on various locations in Antwerp (BE) opened on 14.6.2006

F.T.P.E.S. 1/05

F.T.P.E.S. 1/06

F.T.P.E.S. 1/07

F.T.P.E.S. 1/17

F.T.P.E.S. 1/14

F.T.P.E.S. 1/20

F.T.P.E.S. 1/18

F.T.P.E.S. 1/19

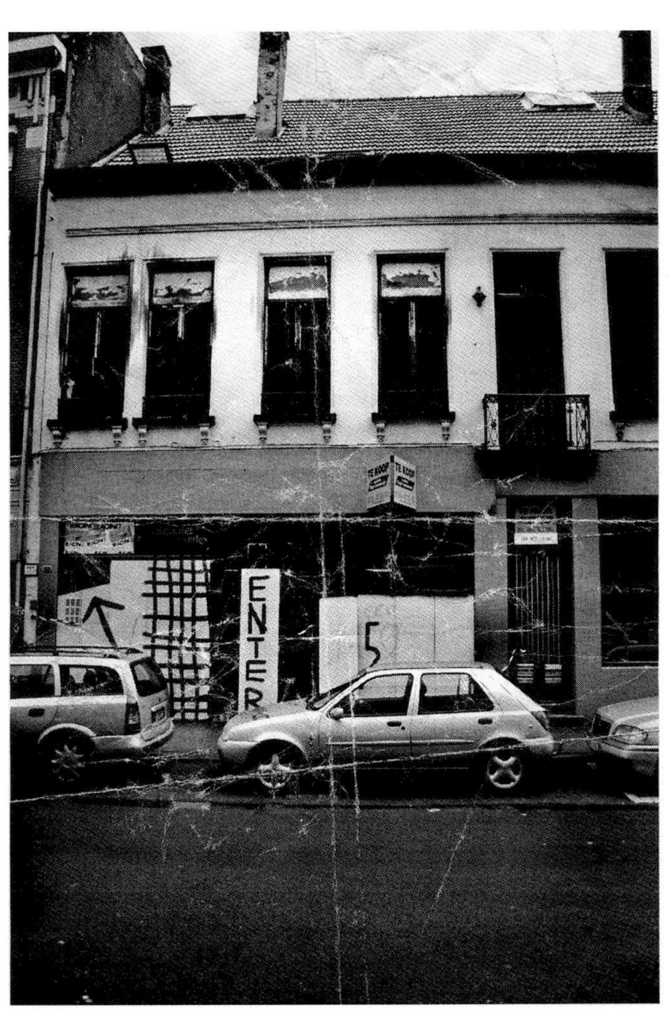
ENTER
5

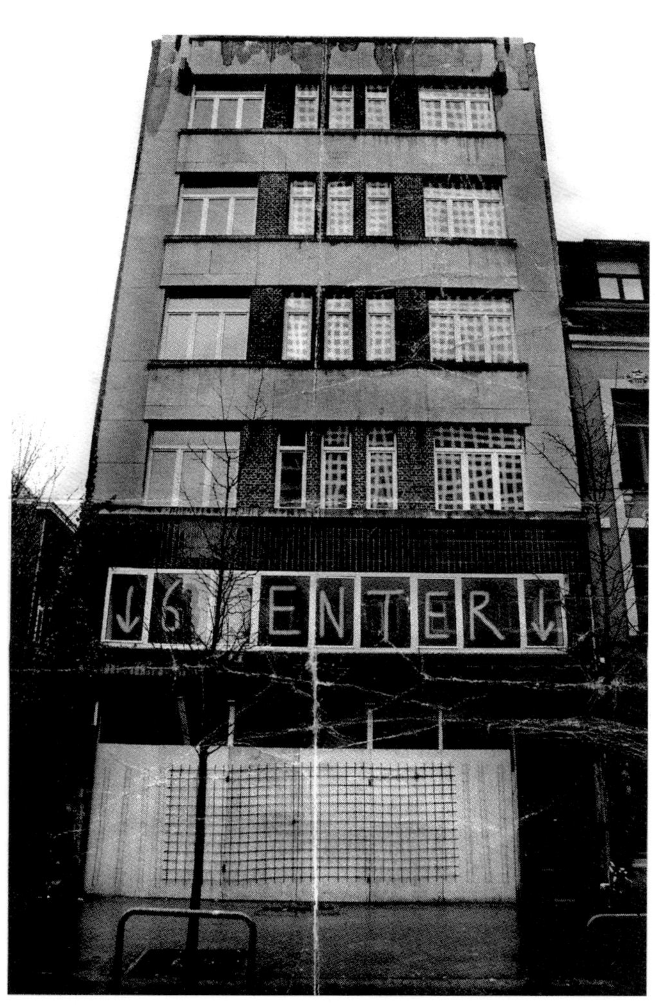
6
ENTER

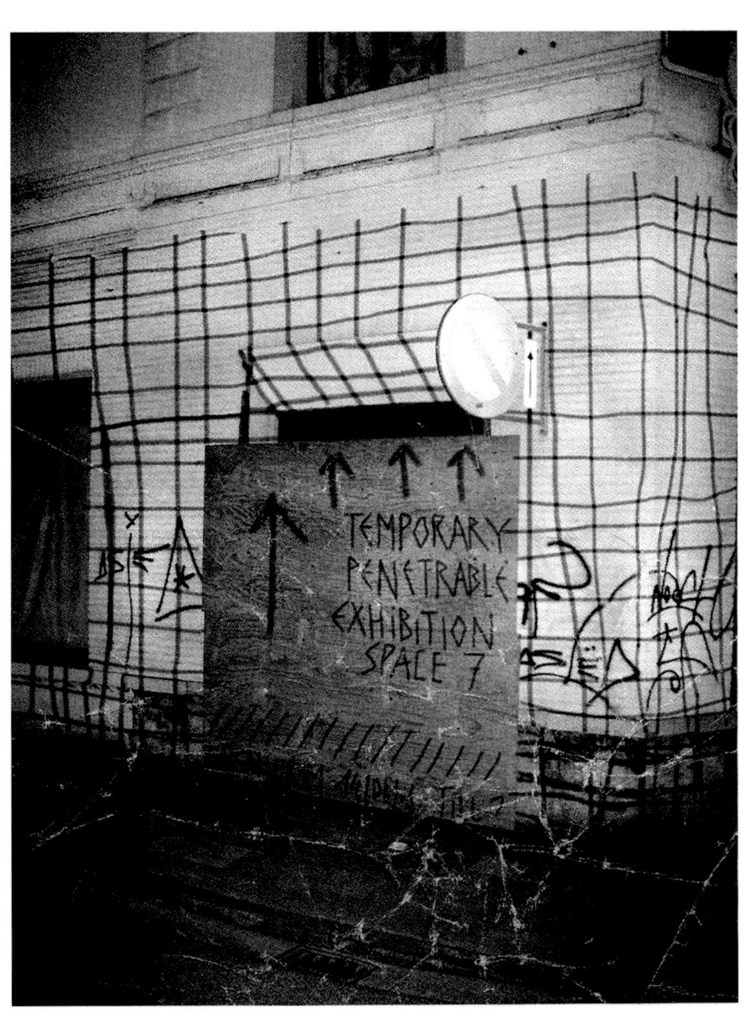
TEMPORARY
PENETRABLE
EXHIBITION
SPACE 7

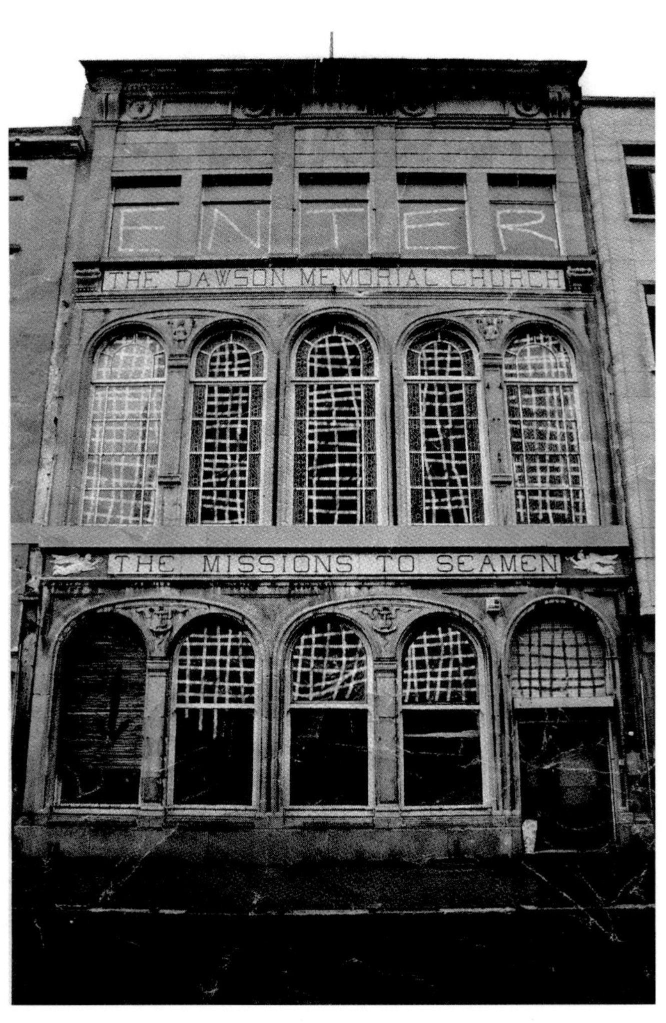
ENTER
THE DAWSON MEMORIAL CHURCH
THE MISSIONS TO SEAMEN

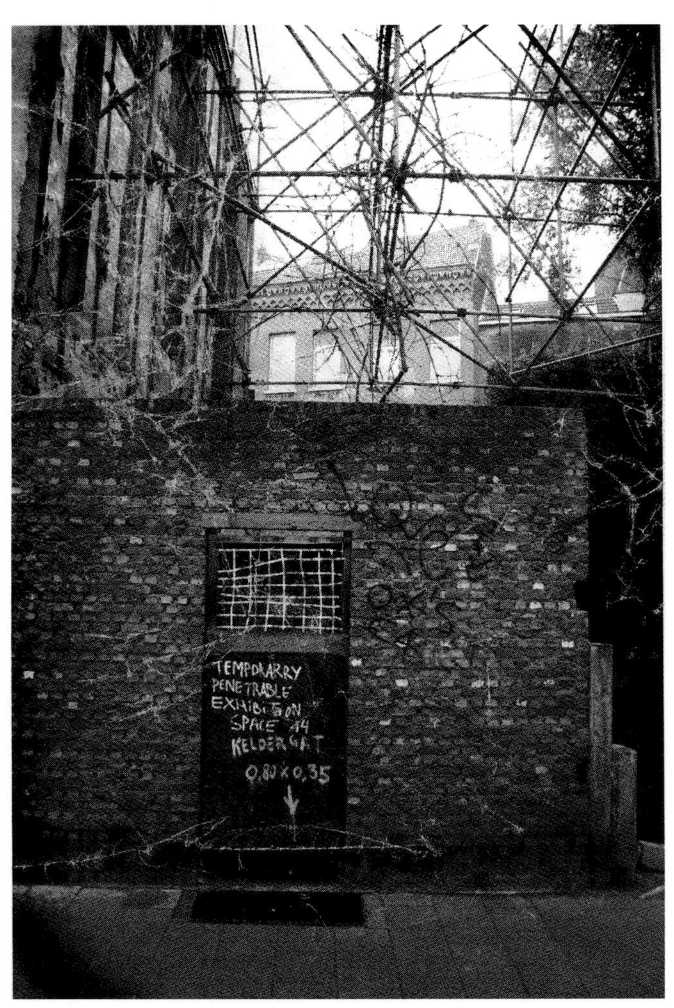
TEMPORARRY
PENETRABLE
EXHIBITION
SPACE 44
KELDERGAT
0,80 x 0,35

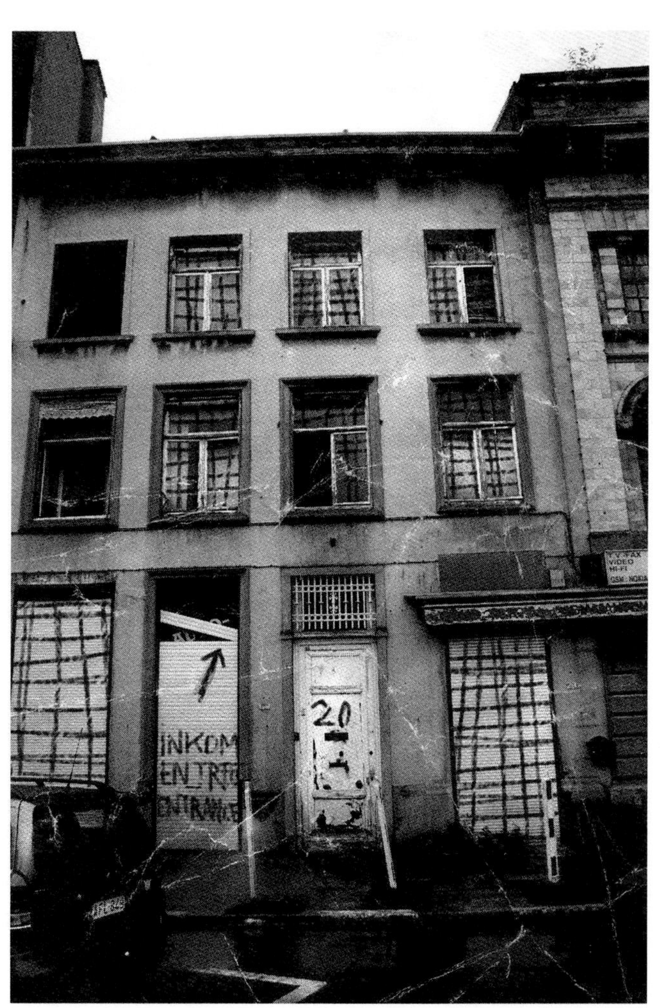
VIDEO
HI-FI
INKOM
20

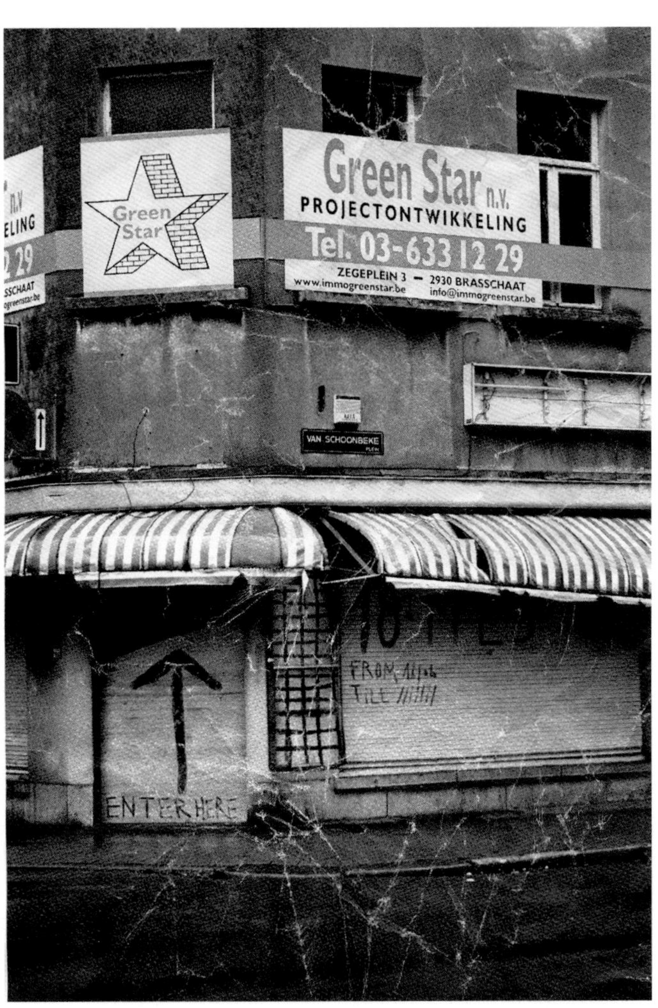
Green Star
Green Star n.v.
PROJECTONTWIKKELING
Tel. 03-633 12 29
ZEGEPLEIN 3 — 2930 BRASSCHAAT
www.immogreenstar.be
info@immogreenstar.be
VAN SCHOONBEKE
ENTER HERE

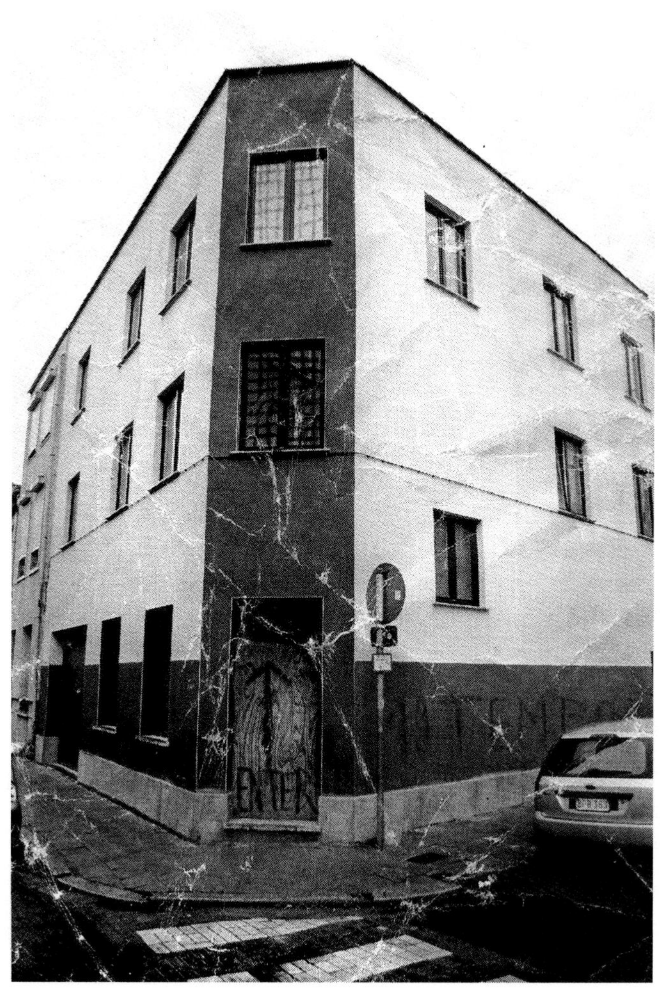
ENTER

'List of Intruders'
for the first 8
T.P.E.S. interventions
silkscreened posters
2005-2014

LIST OF INTRUDERS

OF THE TEMPORARY PENETRABLE EXHIBITION SPACE

NAME///T.P.E.S. 01 DATE OF OPENING///18/11/2005 ADDRESS///KERKSTRAAT, ANTWERP

NAME (OPTIONAL)	SIGNATURE	DATE OF ENTERING

LIST OF INTRUDERS
OF THE TEMPORARY PENETRABLE EXHIBITION SPACE

NAME///T.P.E.S. 02 DATE OF OPENING///25/11/2005 ADDRESS///BEGIJNENSTRAAT, MECHELEN

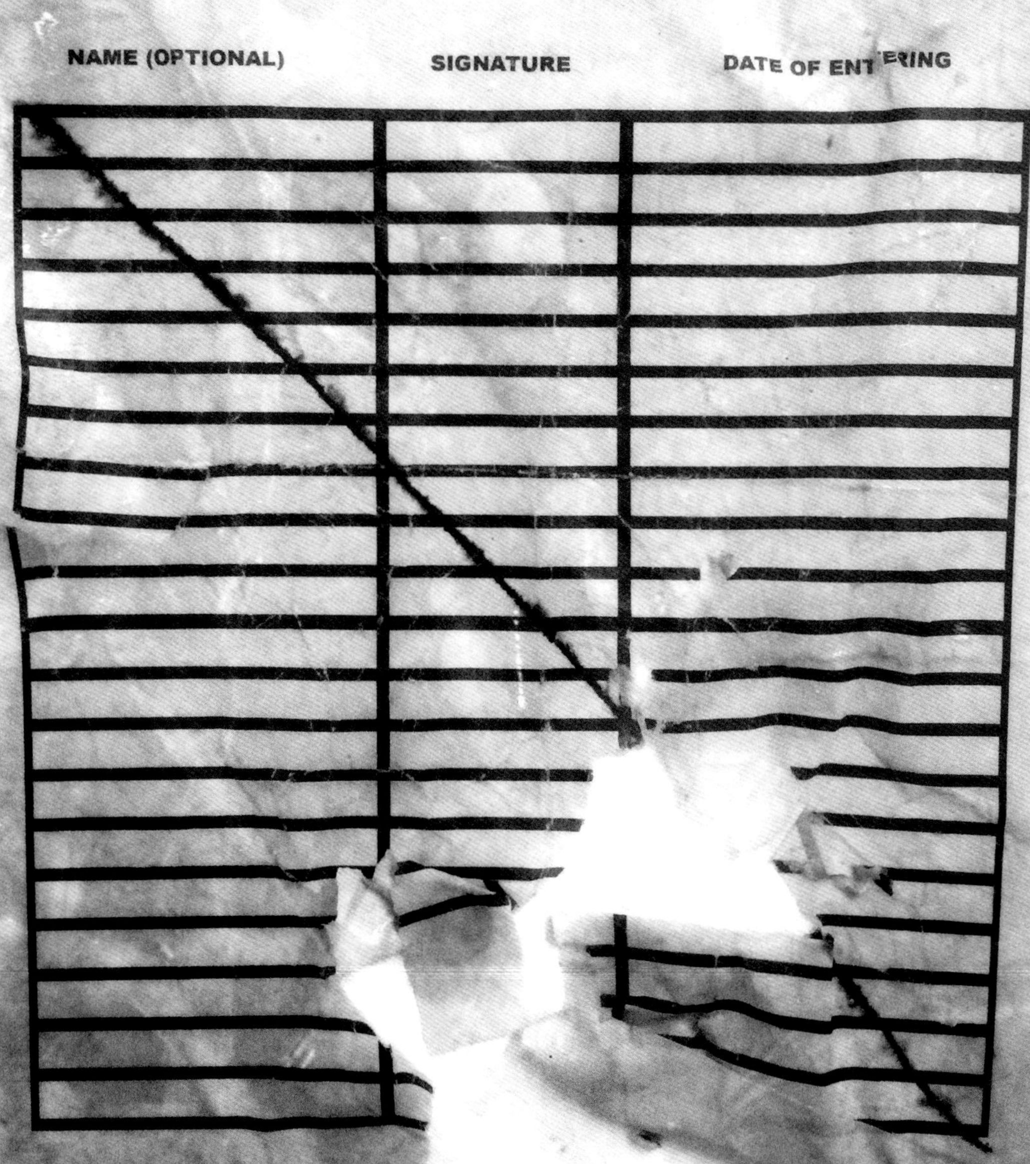

LIST OF INTRUDERS

OF THE TEMPORARY PENETRABLE EXHIBITION SPACE

NAME///T.P.E.S. 03 DATE OF OPENING///26/04/2006 ADDRESS///FACTOR 44 ANTWERP

NAME (OPTIONAL) SIGNATURE DATE OF ENTERING

LIST OF INTRUDERS
OF THE TEMPORARY PENETRABLE EXHIBITION SPACE

NAME///T.P.E.S. 0[illegible] 4 DATE OF OPENING///[illegible] 9/10/08 ADDRESS///[illegible] [illegible]HIESTRAAT ROTTERDAM

NAME (OPTIONAL) SIGNATURE DATE OF ENTERING

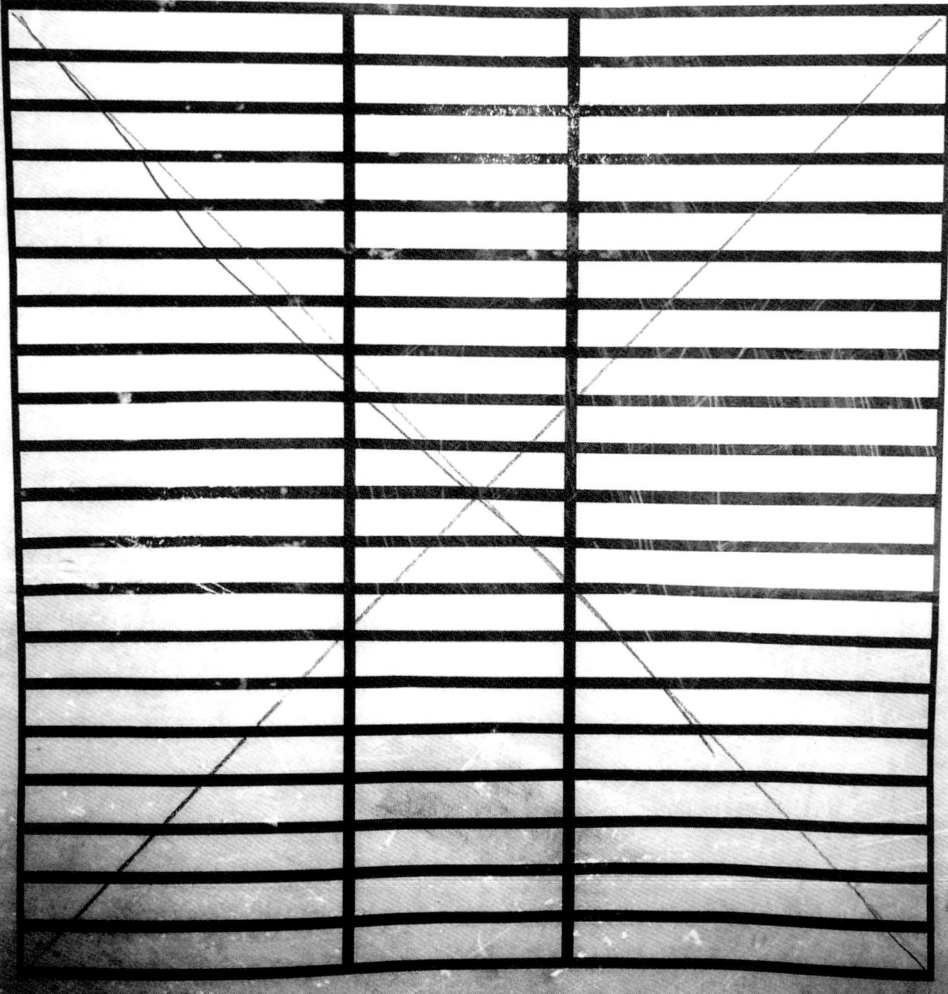

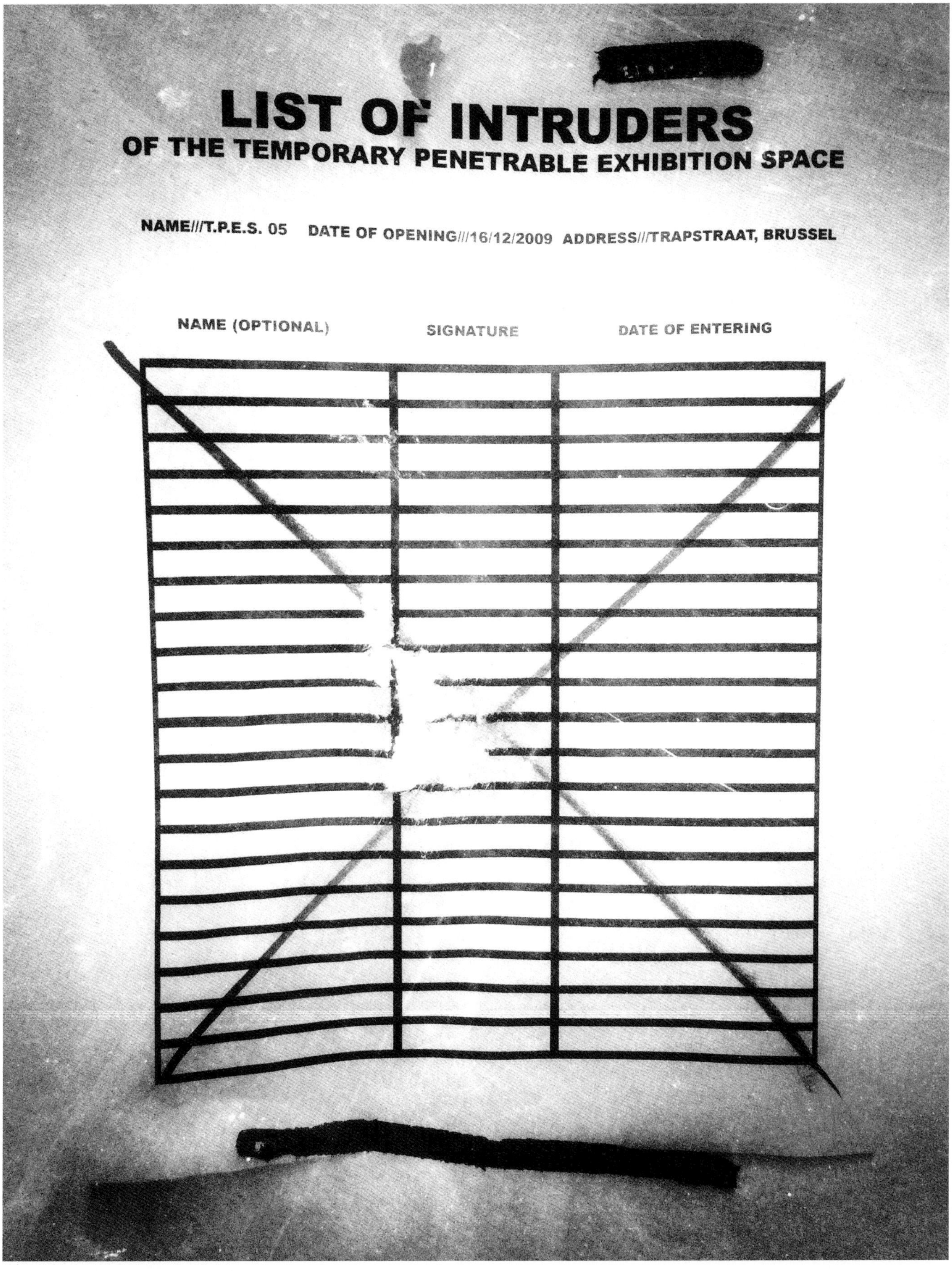

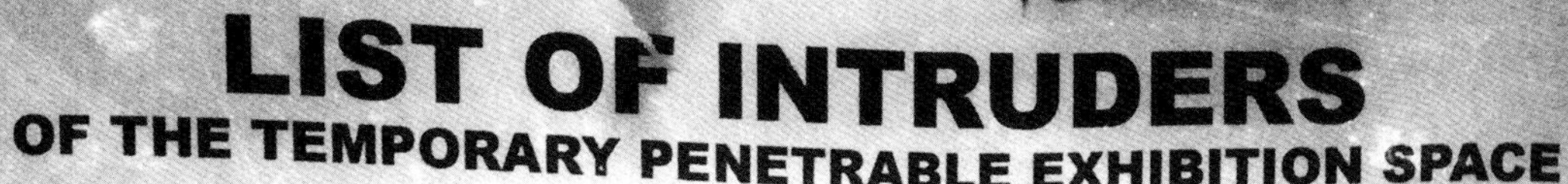

OF THE TEMPORARY PENETRABLE EXHIBITION SPACE

NAME///T.P.E.S. 05 DATE OF OPENING///16/12/2009 ADDRESS///TRAPSTRAAT, BRUSSEL

NAME (OPTIONAL)	SIGNATURE	DATE OF ENTERING

LIST OF INTRUDERS

OF THE TEMPORARY PENETRABLE EXHIBITION SPACE

NAME///T.P.E.S. 06 DATE OF OPENING/// 25/6/11 ADDRESS/// FREESTATE II OOSTEND

NAME (OPTIONAL) **SIGNATURE** **DATE OF ENTERING**

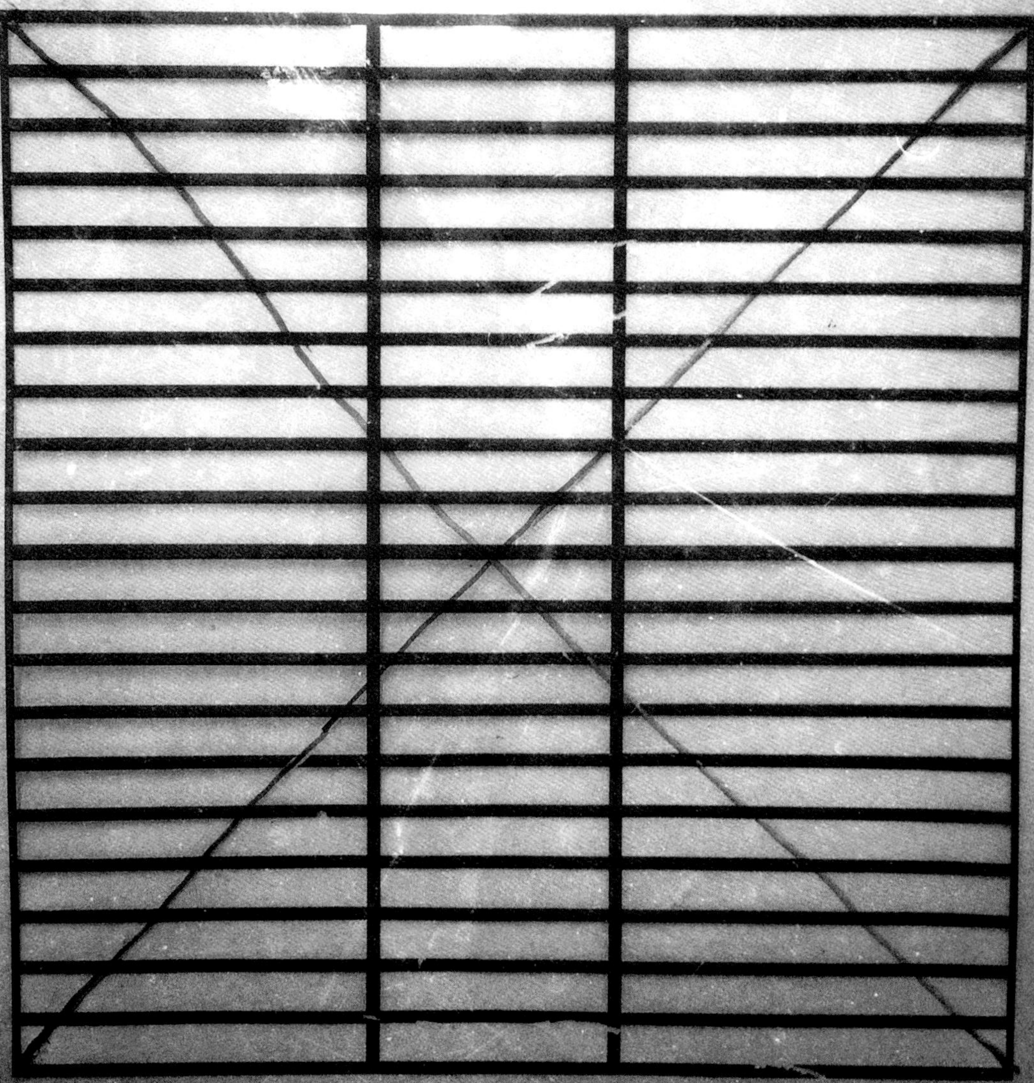

LIST OF INTRUDERS

OF THE TEMPORARY PENETRABLE EXHIBITION SPACE

NAME///T.P.E.S. 07(2) DATE OF OPENING///07/06 ADDRESS/// 52295667N132224090

2012 RAUMEXPERIMENTE GLEISSDREIECK STATION

NAME (OPTIONAL)	SIGNATURE	DATE OF ENTERING

LIST OF INTRUDERS

OF THE TEMPORARY PENETRABLE EXHIBITION SPACE

NAME///T.P.E.S. 07(3) DATE OF OPENING///07/05/2013 ADDRESS/// 50244445N042442900

(B)

NAME (OPTIONAL)	SIGNATURE	DATE OF ENTERING

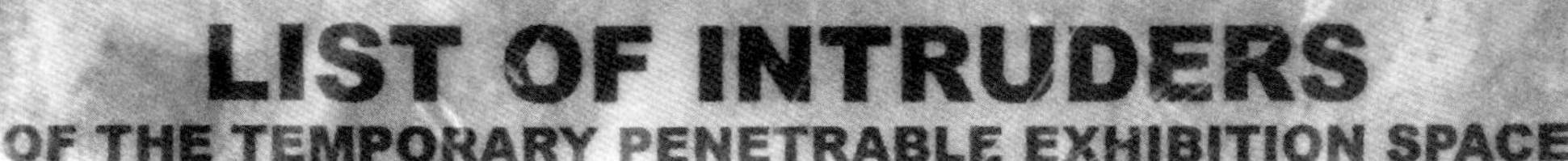

MS///T.P.E.S. 08 DATE OF OPENING///21/03/2014 ADDRESS/// 50391056N053514430

NAME (OPTIONAL)	SIGNATURE	DATE OF ENTERING

T.P.E.S. 3
‘BASE A’ at
Factor 44, Antwerp
starting point
for visiting the 7
opened spaces
part of T.P.E.S. 3

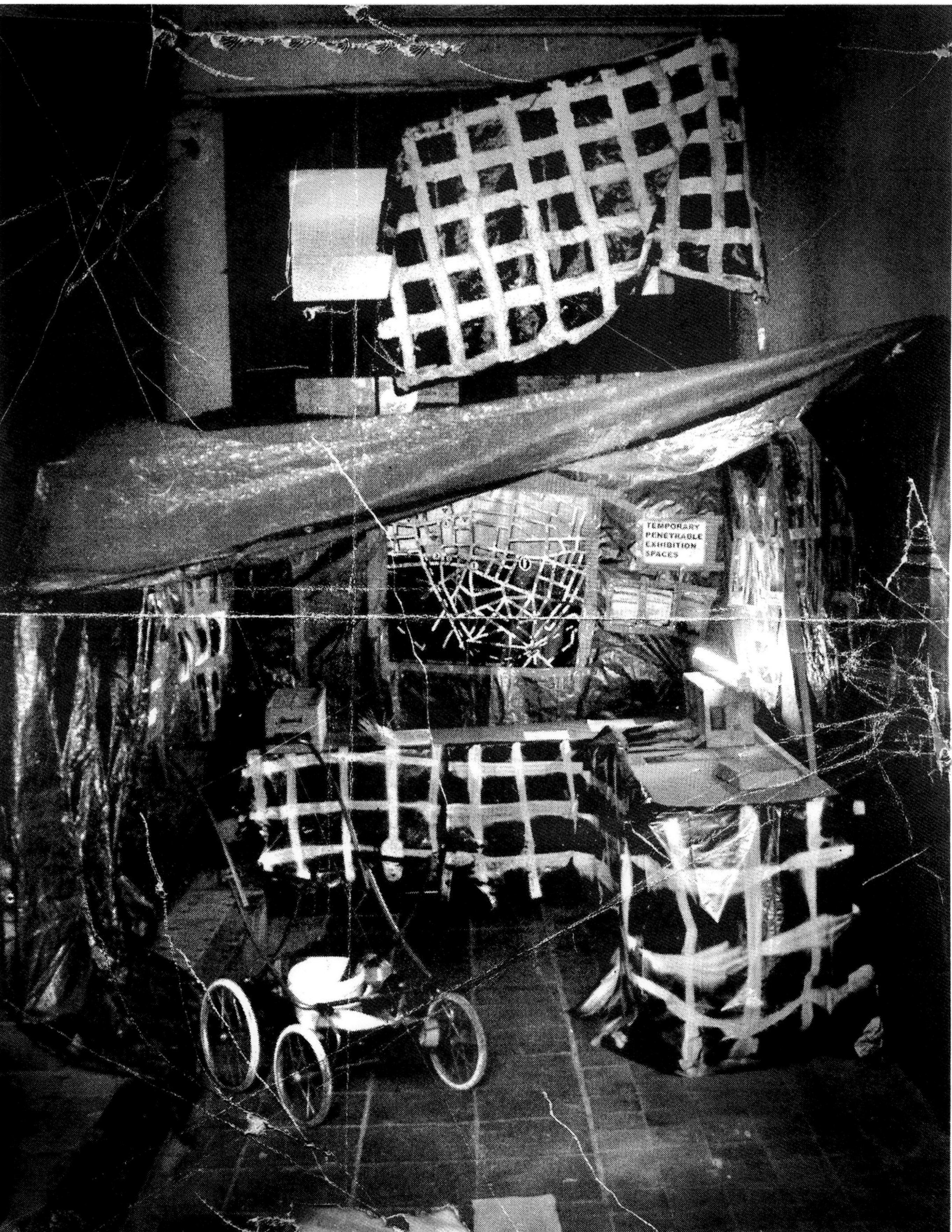
TEMPORARY
PENETRABLE
EXHIBITION
SPACES

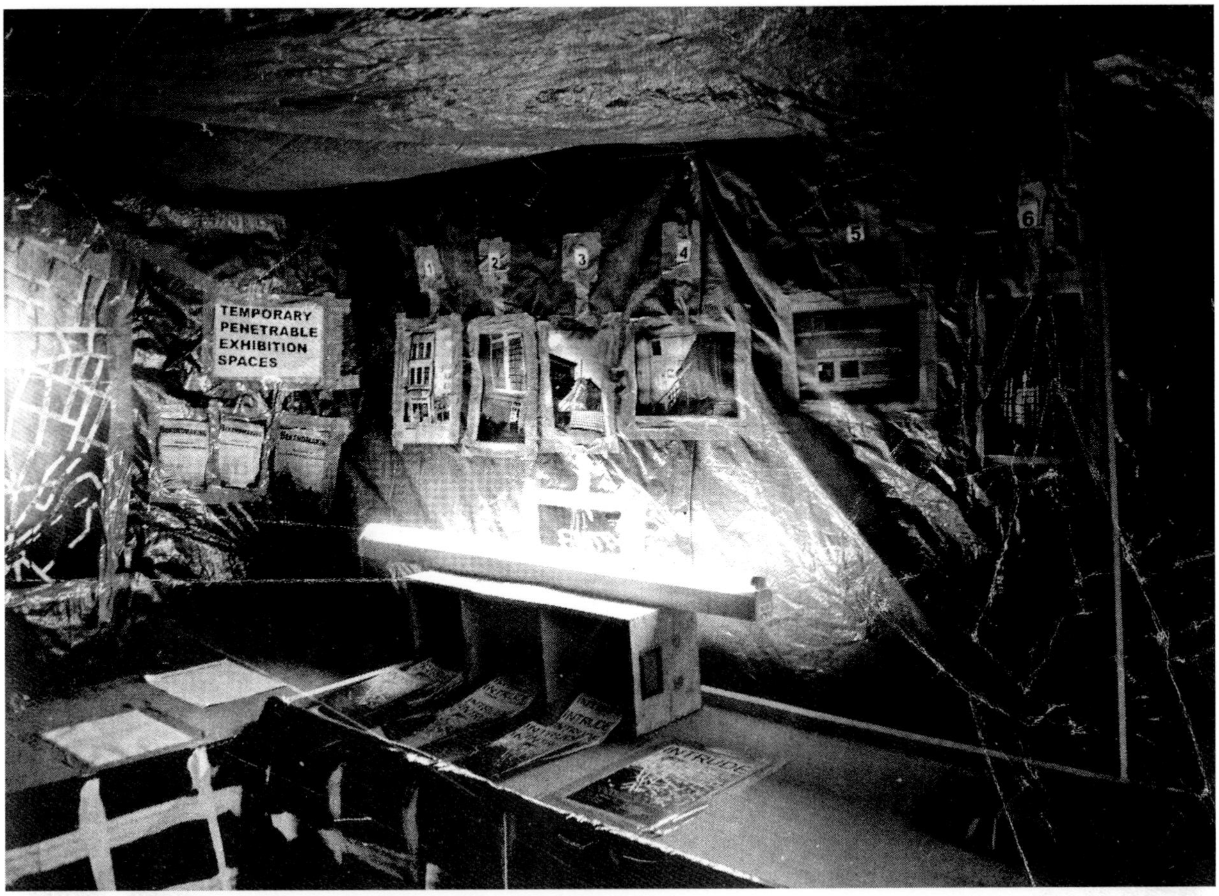

TEMPORARY
PENETRABLE
EXHIBITION
SPACES
BEKENDMAKING

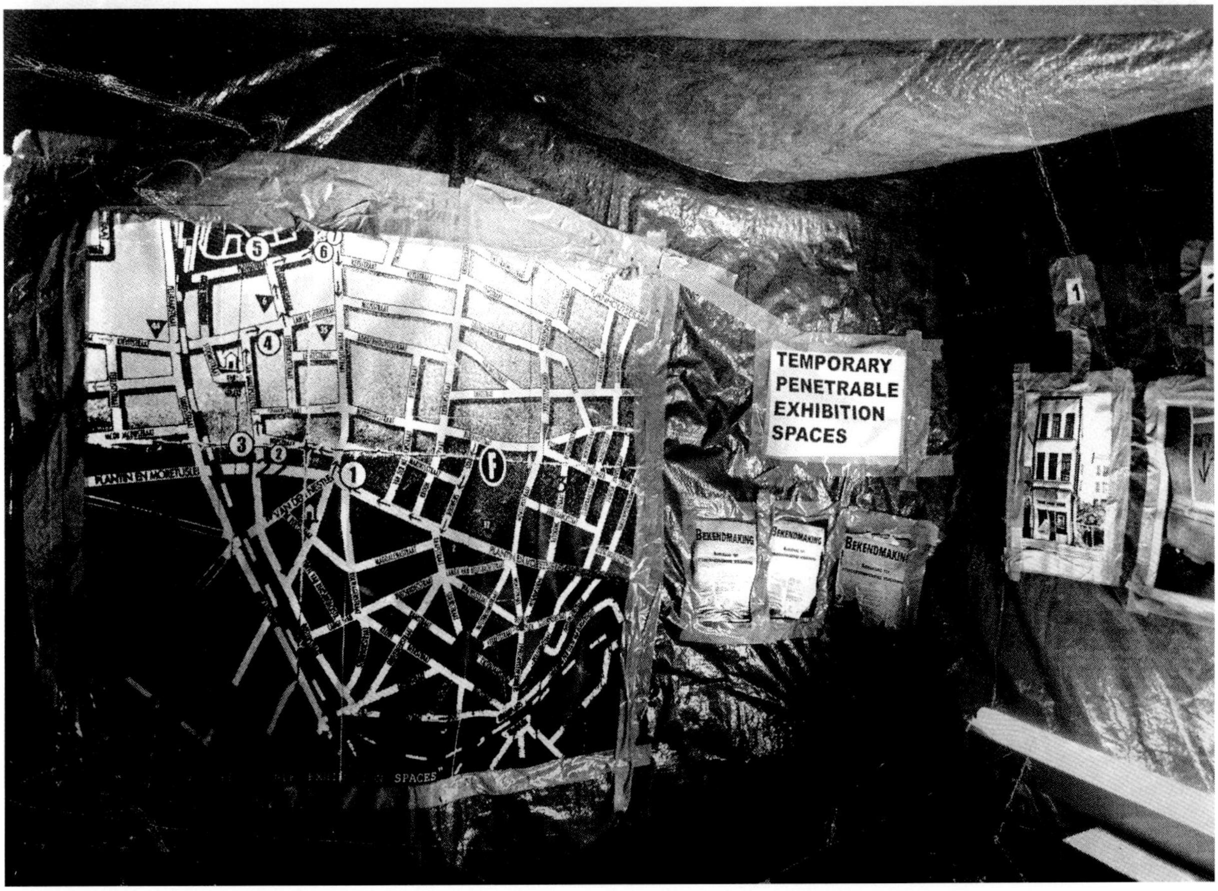

TEMPORARY
PENETRABLE
EXHIBITION
SPACES
BEKENDMAKING
BEKENDMAKING
BEKENDMAKING

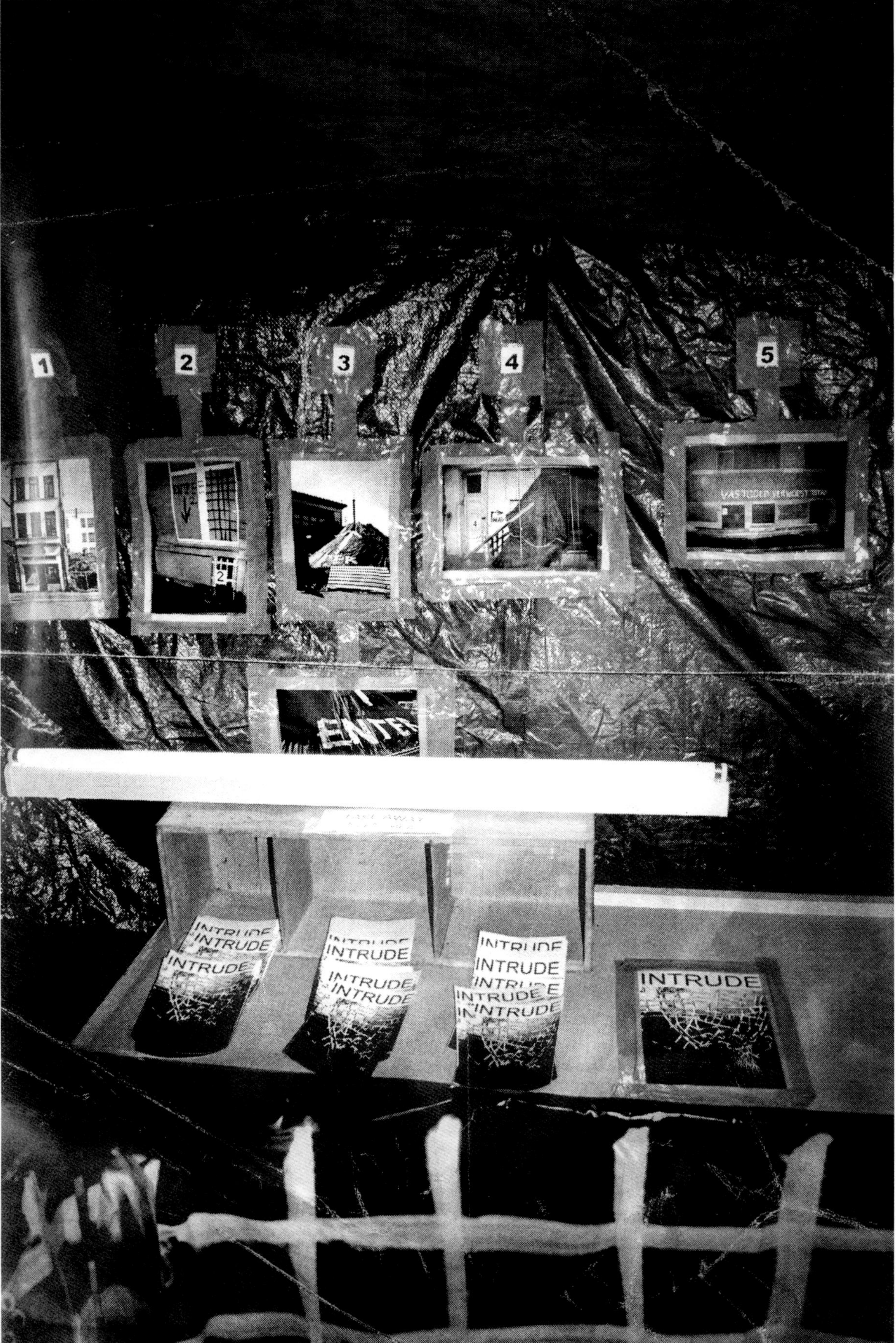
1
2
3
4
5
ENTER
INTRUDE
INTRUDE
INTRUDE
INTRUDE
INTRUDE
INTRUDE
INTRUDE
INTRUDE
INTRUDE

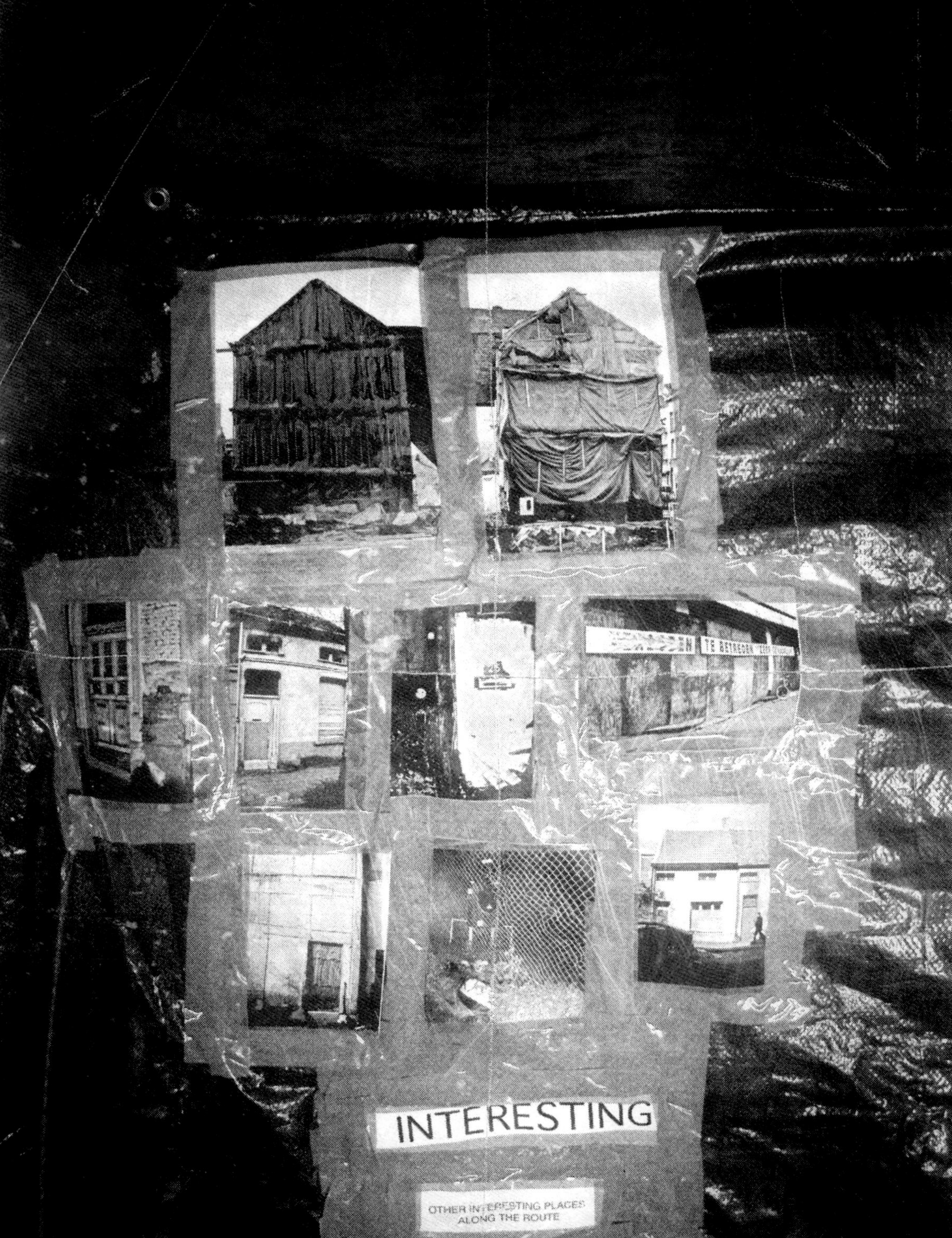
INTERESTING
OTHER INTERESTING PLACES
ALONG THE ROUTE

flyers and leaflets for the first 7 T.P.E.S. interventions 2005-2011

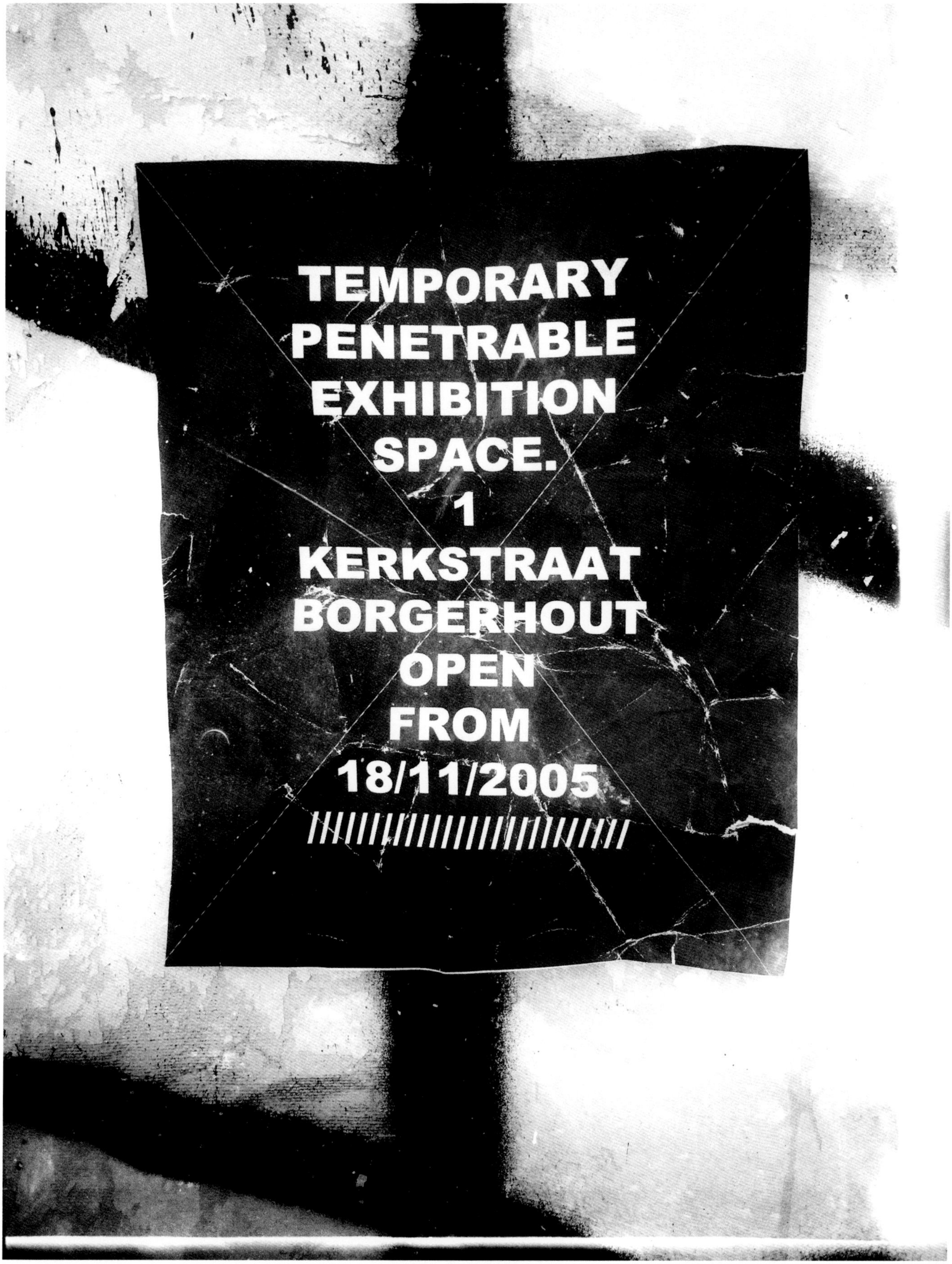

TEMPORARY
PENETRABLE
EXHIBITION
SPACE.
1
KERKSTRAAT
BORGERHOUT
OPEN
FROM
18/11/2005

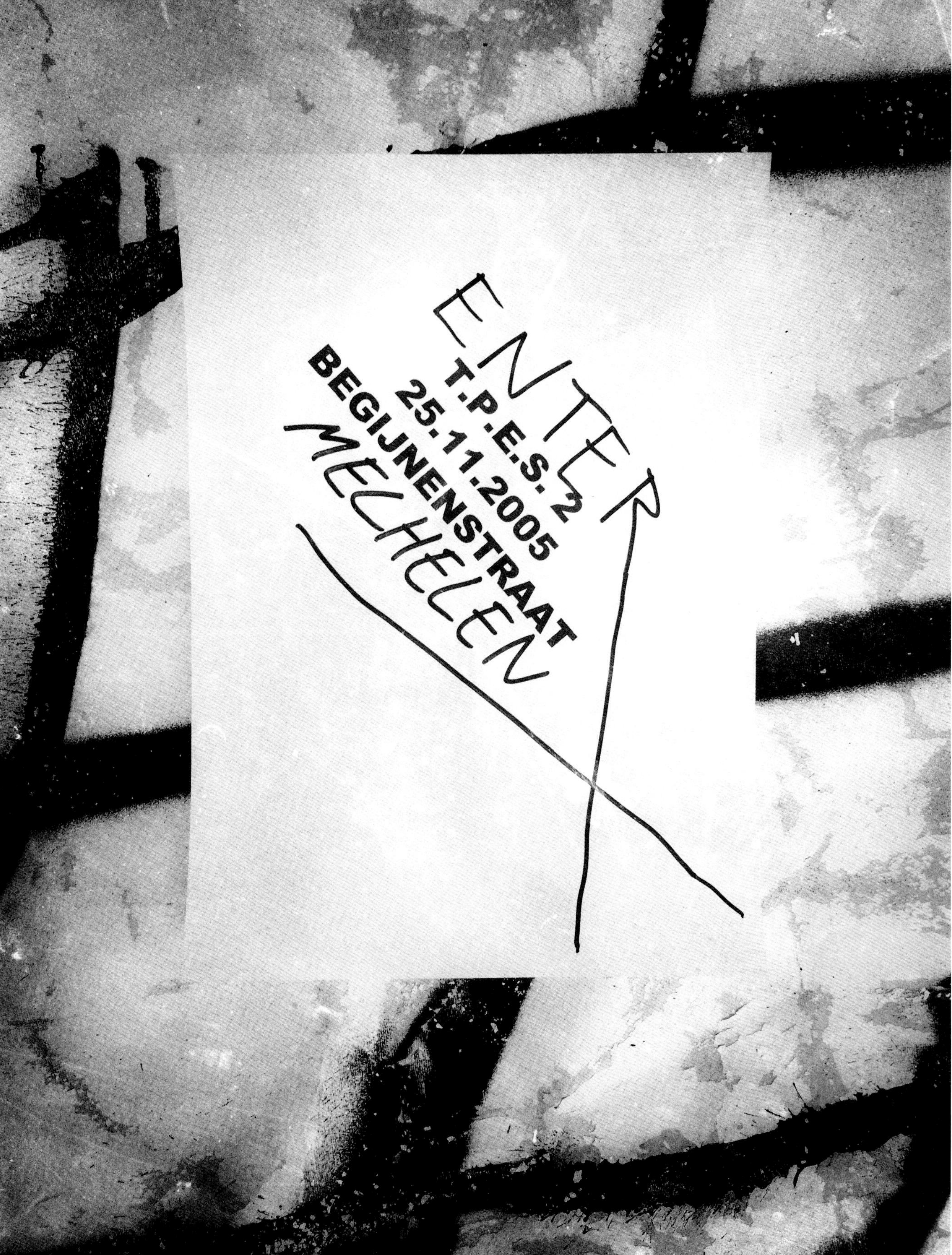
ENTER
T.P.E.S. 2
25.11.2005
BEGIJNENSTRAAT
MECHELEN

INTRUDE

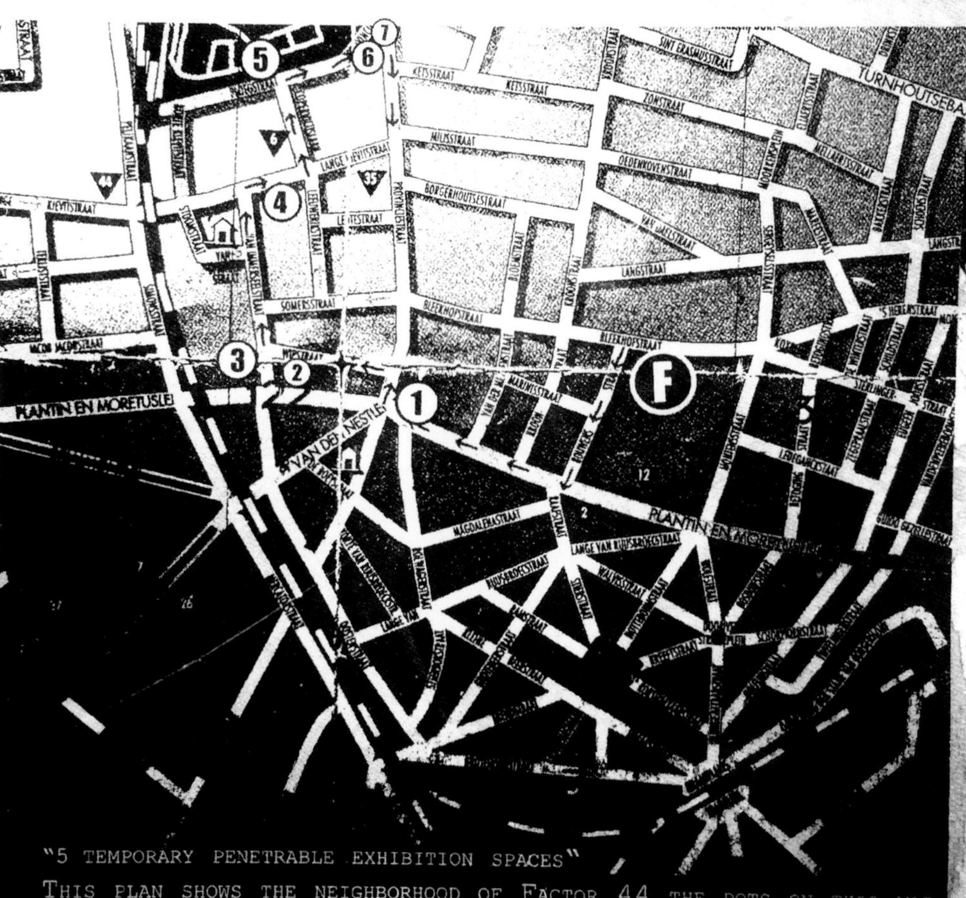

"5 TEMPORARY PENETRABLE EXHIBITION SPACES"

THIS PLAN SHOWS THE NEIGHBORHOOD OF FACTOR 44 THE DOTS ON THIS MAP INDICATE THE LOCATION OF INTERVENTIONS.

1 PLANTIN EN MORETUSLEI 97
2 WIPSTRAAT 37
3 VAN IMMERSEELSTRAAT
4 LANGE KIEVITSTRAAT 88
5 PLOEGSTRAAT
6 PLOEGSTRAAT-PROVINCIESTRAAT
7 PROVINCIESTRAAT
8 ++++++++++

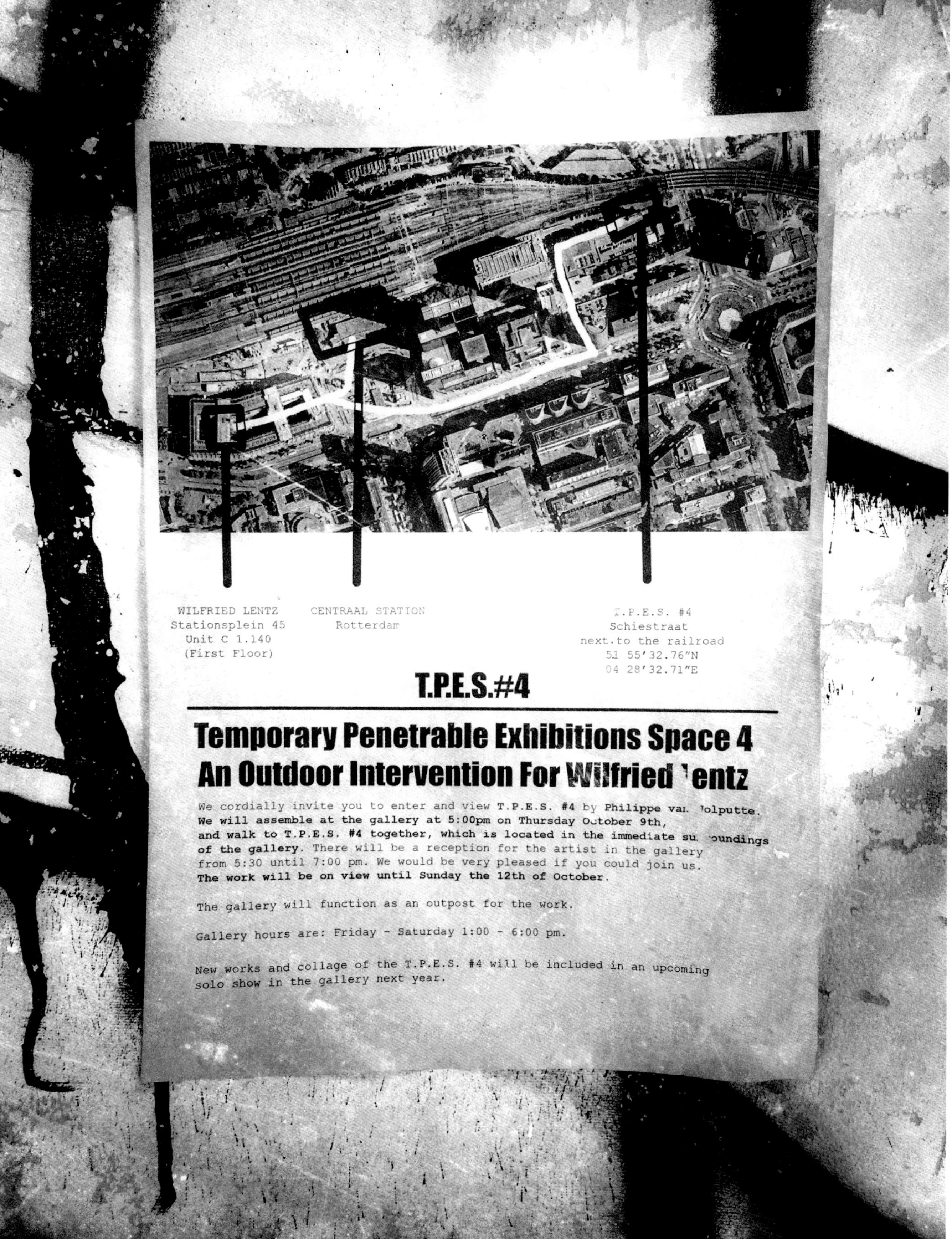

WILFRIED LENTZ
Stationsplein 45
Unit C 1.140
(First Floor)
CENTRAAL STATION
Rotterdam
T.P.E.S. #4
Schiestraat
next.to the railroad
51 55'32.76"N
04 28'32.71"E
T.P.E.S.#4
Temporary Penetrable Exhibitions Space 4
An Outdoor Intervention For Wilfried Lentz
We cordially invite you to enter and view T.P.E.S. #4 by Philippe van Wolputte.
We will assemble at the gallery at 5:00pm on Thursday October 9th,
and walk to T.P.E.S. #4 together, which is located in the immediate surroundings
of the gallery. There will be a reception for the artist in the gallery
from 5:30 until 7:00 pm. We would be very pleased if you could join us.
The work will be on view until Sunday the 12th of October.
The gallery will function as an outpost for the work.
Gallery hours are: Friday - Saturday 1:00 - 6:00 pm.
New works and collage of the T.P.E.S. #4 will be included in an upcoming
solo show in the gallery next year.

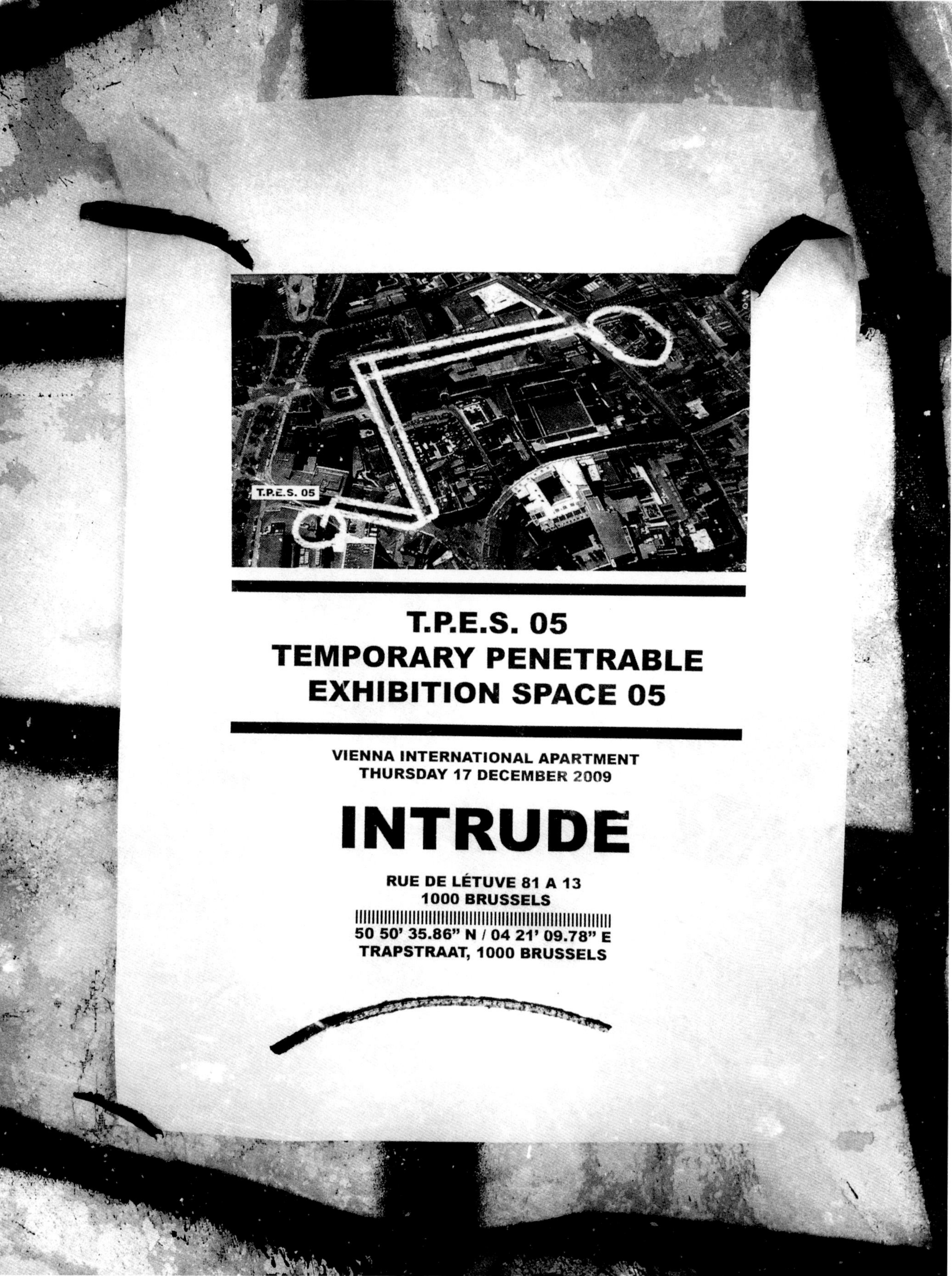
T.P.E.S. 05
T.P.E.S. 05
TEMPORARY PENETRABLE
EXHIBITION SPACE 05
VIENNA INTERNATIONAL APARTMENT
THURSDAY 17 DECEMBER 2009
INTRUDE
RUE DE LÉTUVE 81 A 13
1000 BRUSSELS
50 50' 35.86" N / 04 21' 09.78" E
TRAPSTRAAT, 1000 BRUSSELS

TEMPORARY PENETRABLE
EXHIBITION SPACE SIX
25/6/2011
FREESTATE
OOSTEND

banners for the first 8
T.P.E.S. interventions
2005-2014

ENTER
HERE

T.P.E.O.2
OPEN FROM TILL
2.5 11 05
BEGIJNENSTRAAT
2000 MECHELEN

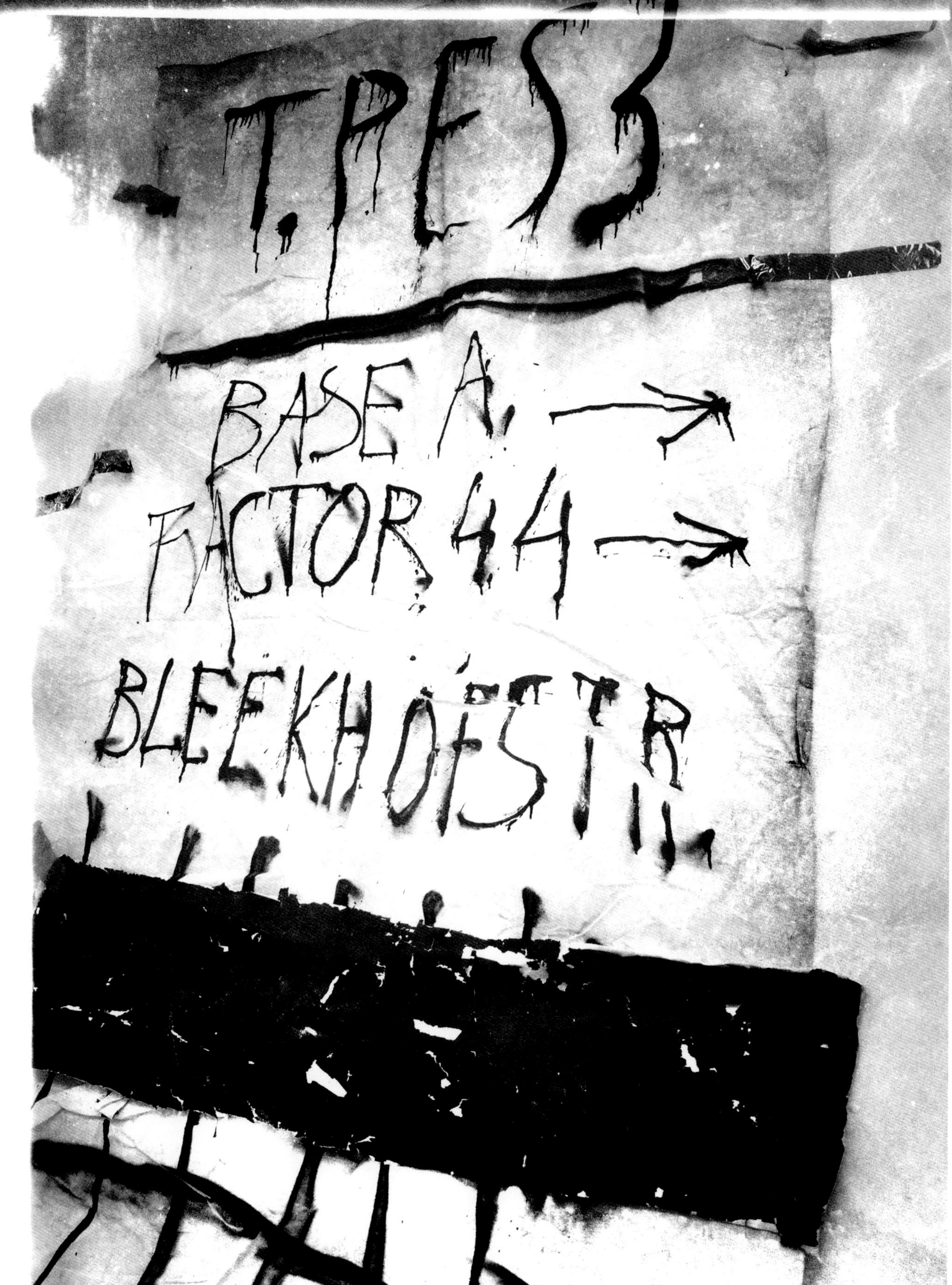
BASE A. →
FACTOR 44 →
BLEEKHOFSTR

TPES4
OPEN
FROM

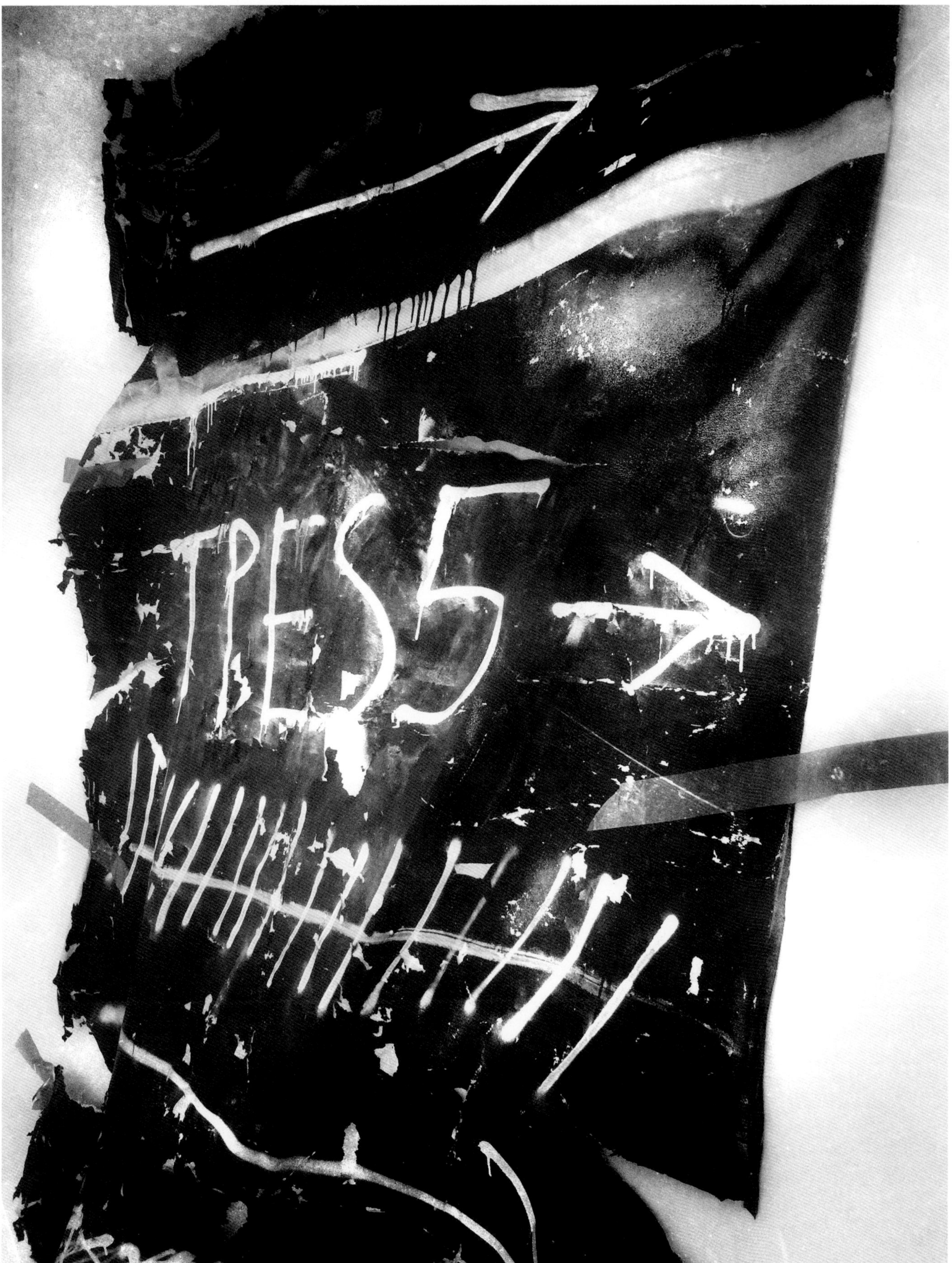
TPES5

TPES6
FREESTATE

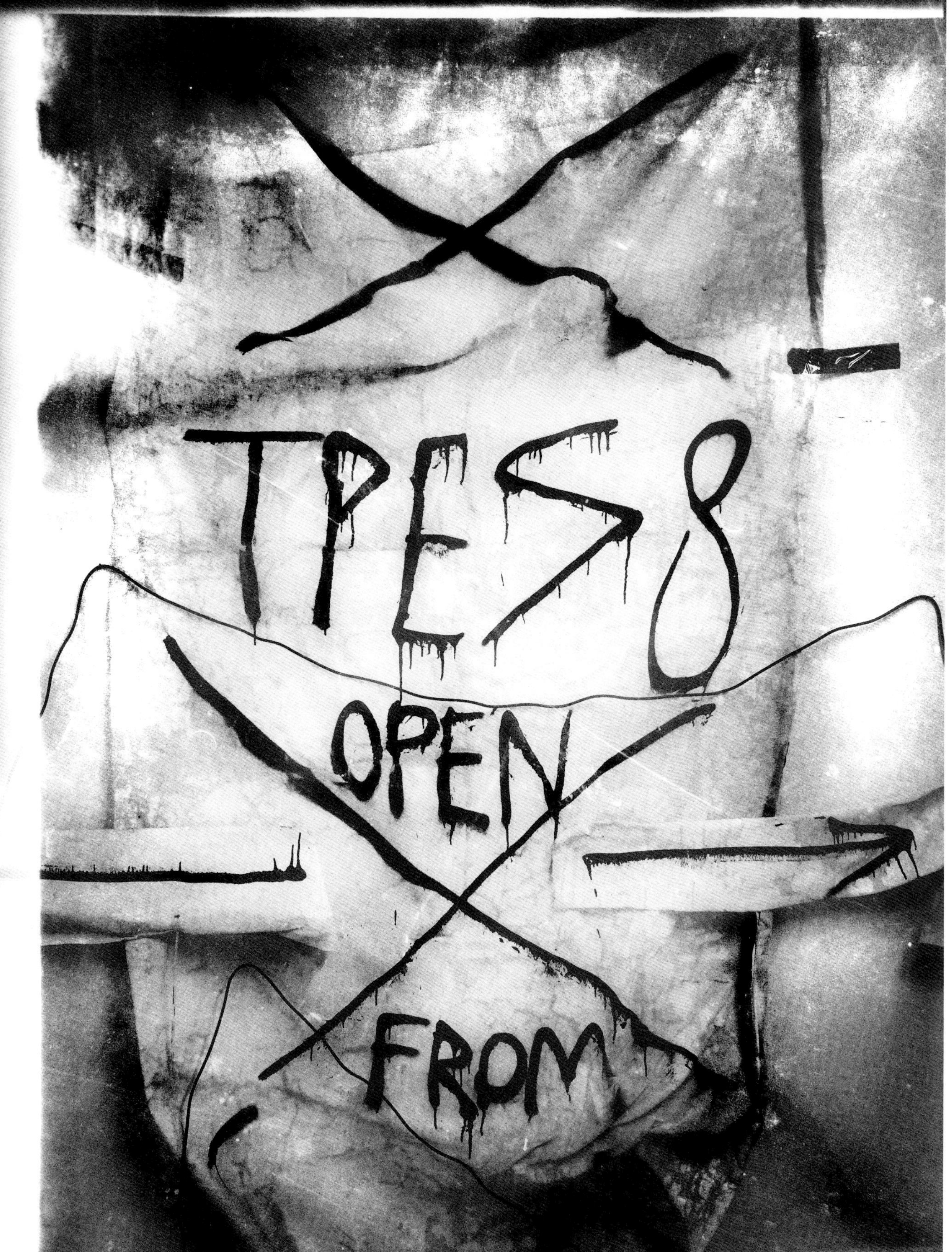
OPEN
FROM

close ups of banners
and spray painted grids
for Temporary Penetrable
Exhibition Spaces
impasto-gel, ink,
aluminium
160 x 120 cm
2015

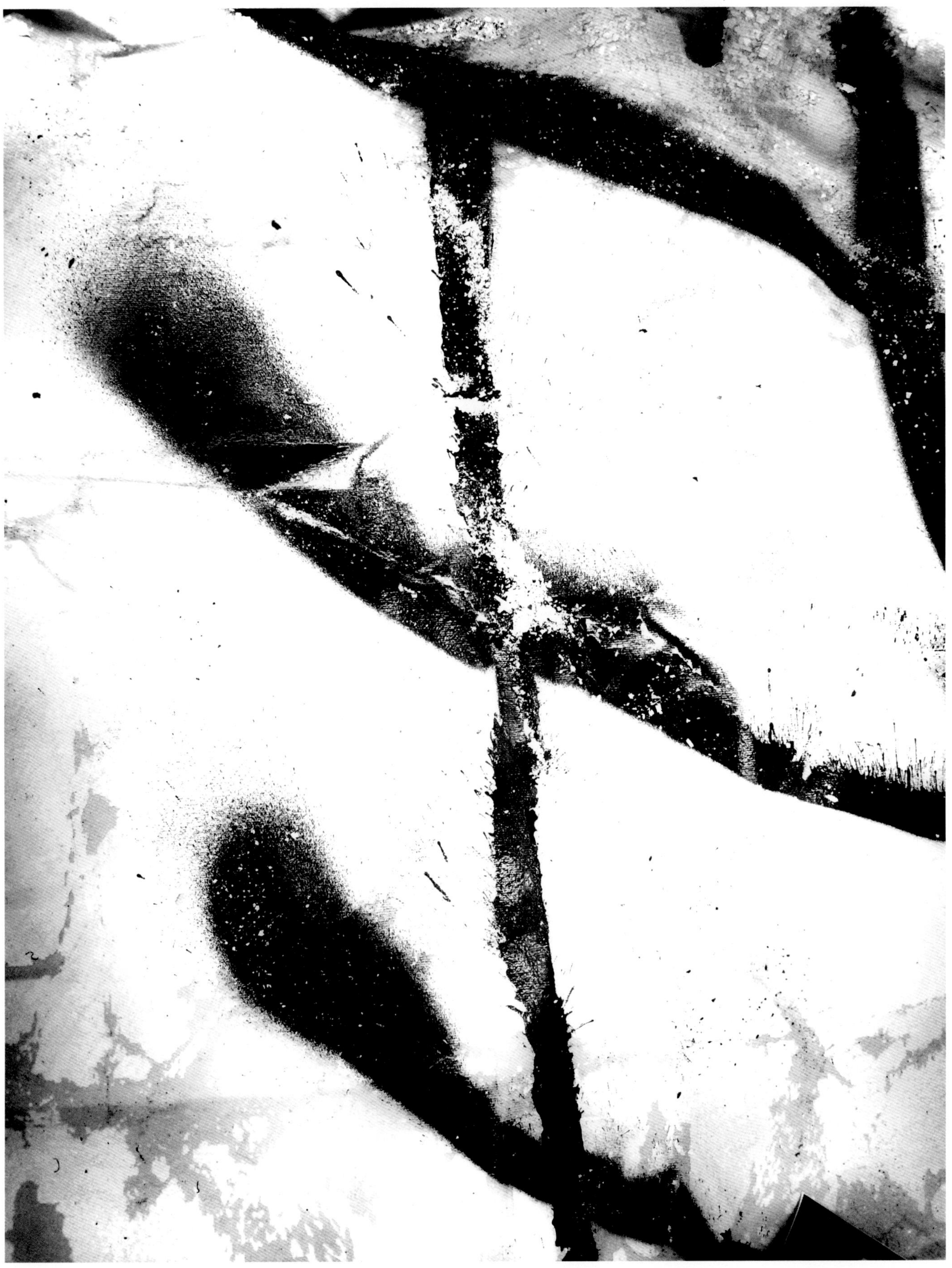

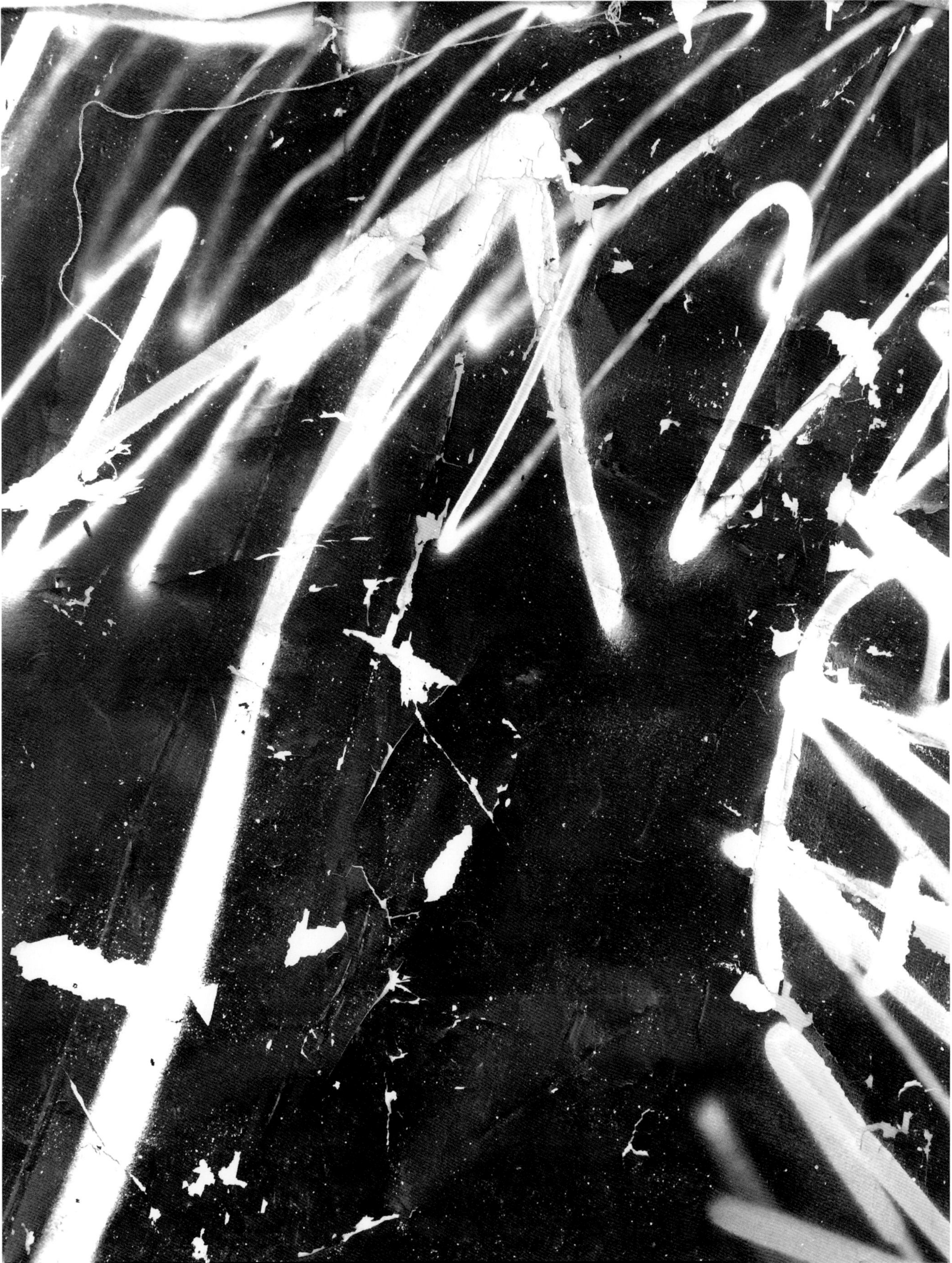

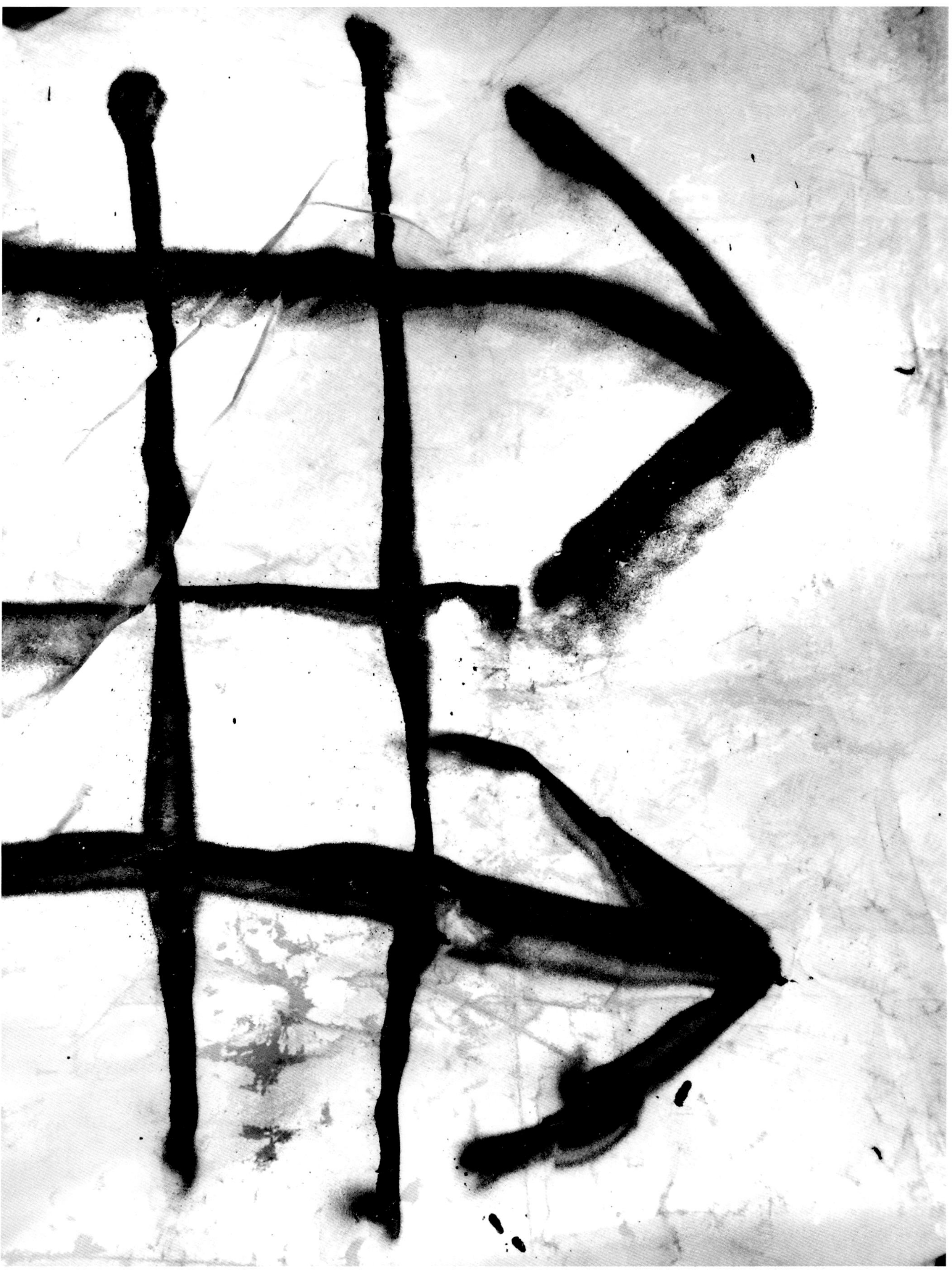

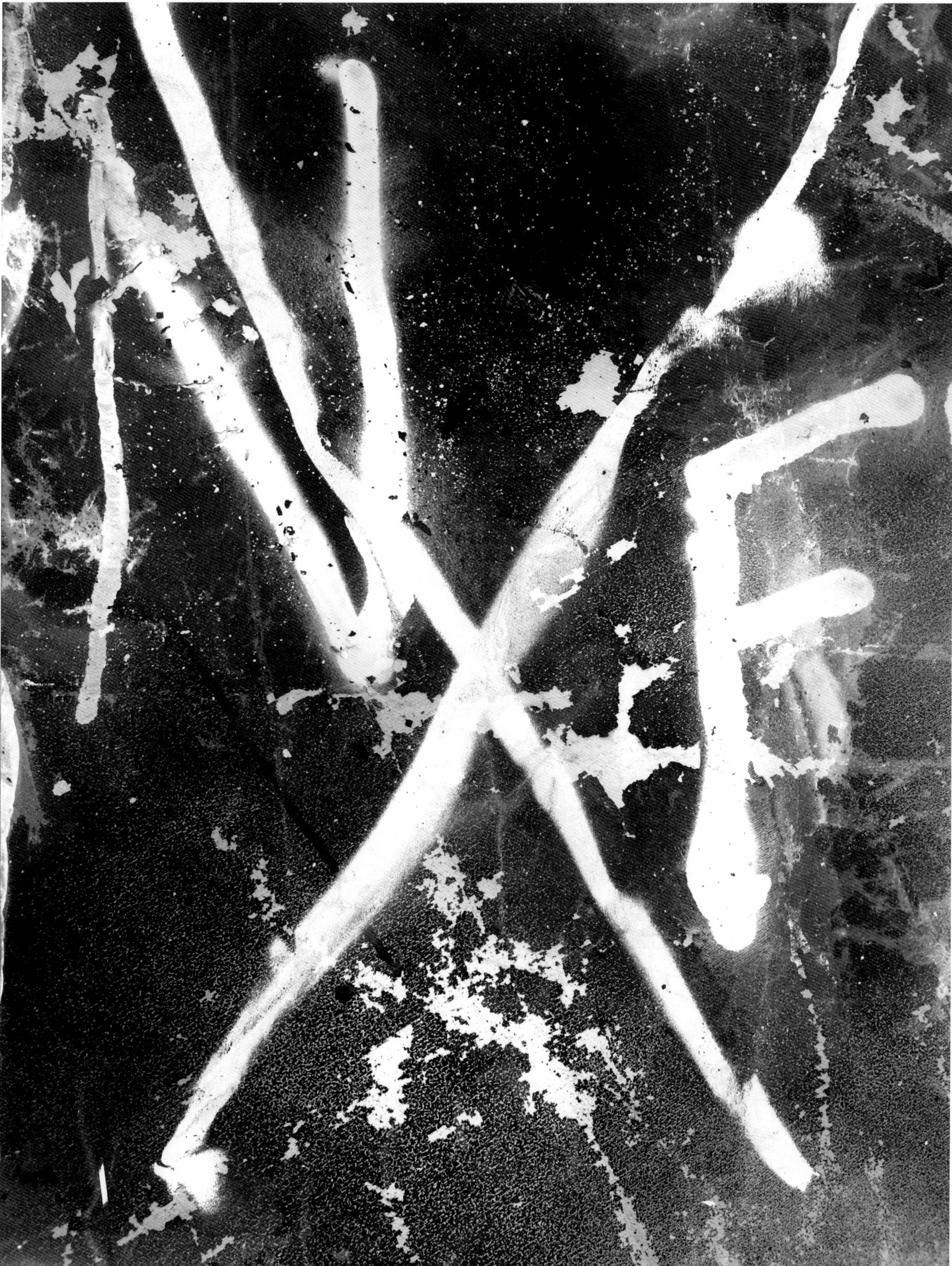

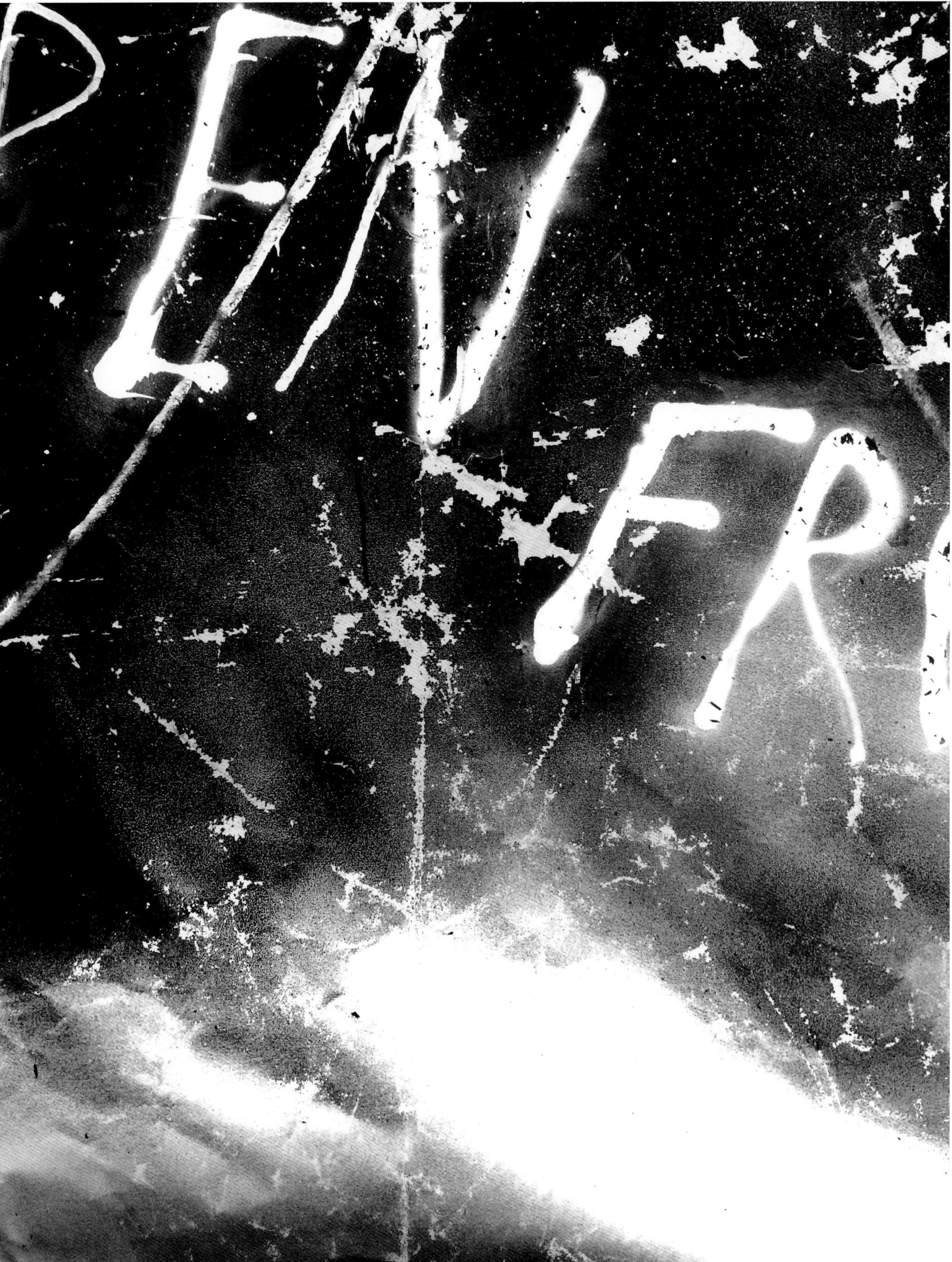
EN
FR

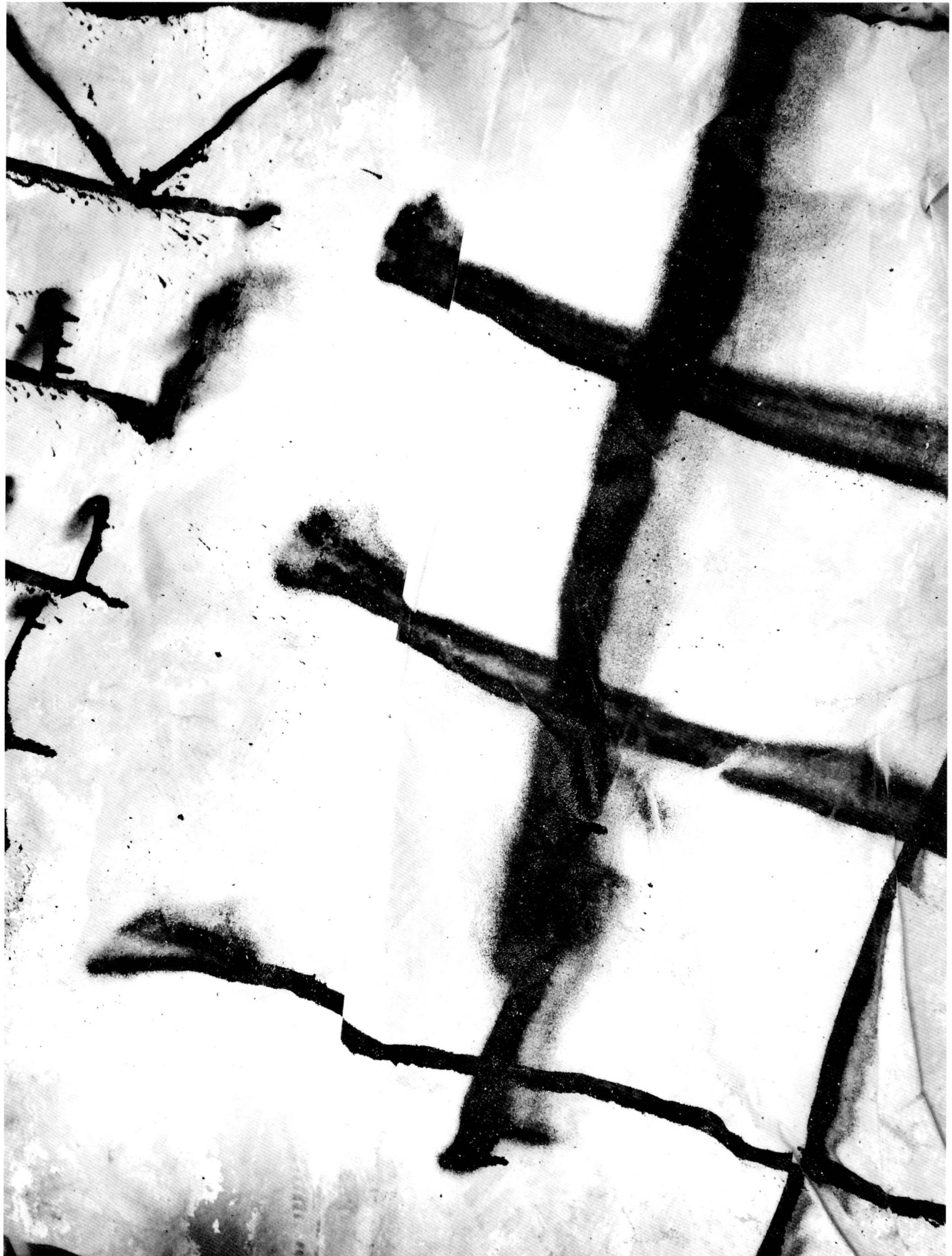

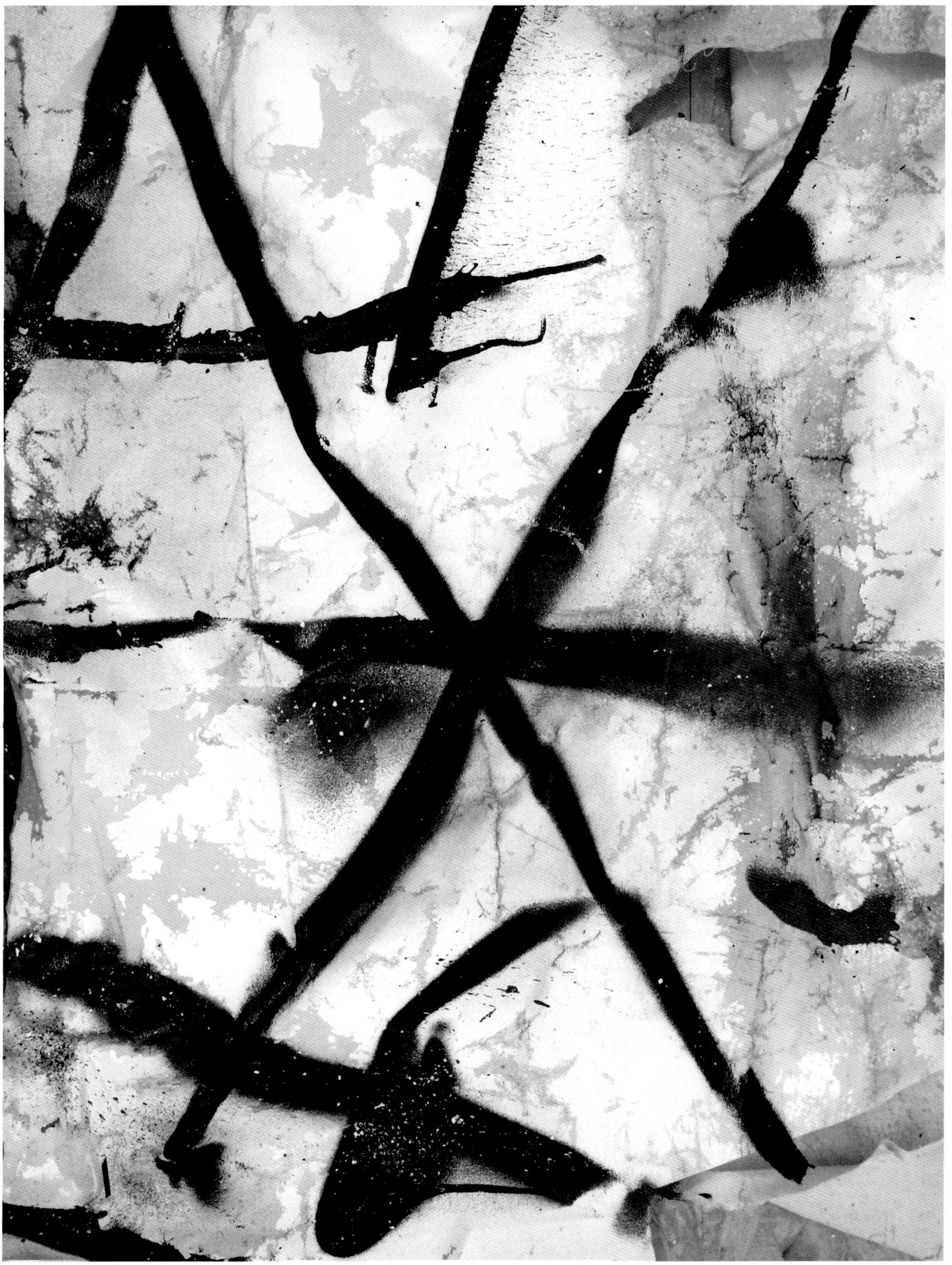

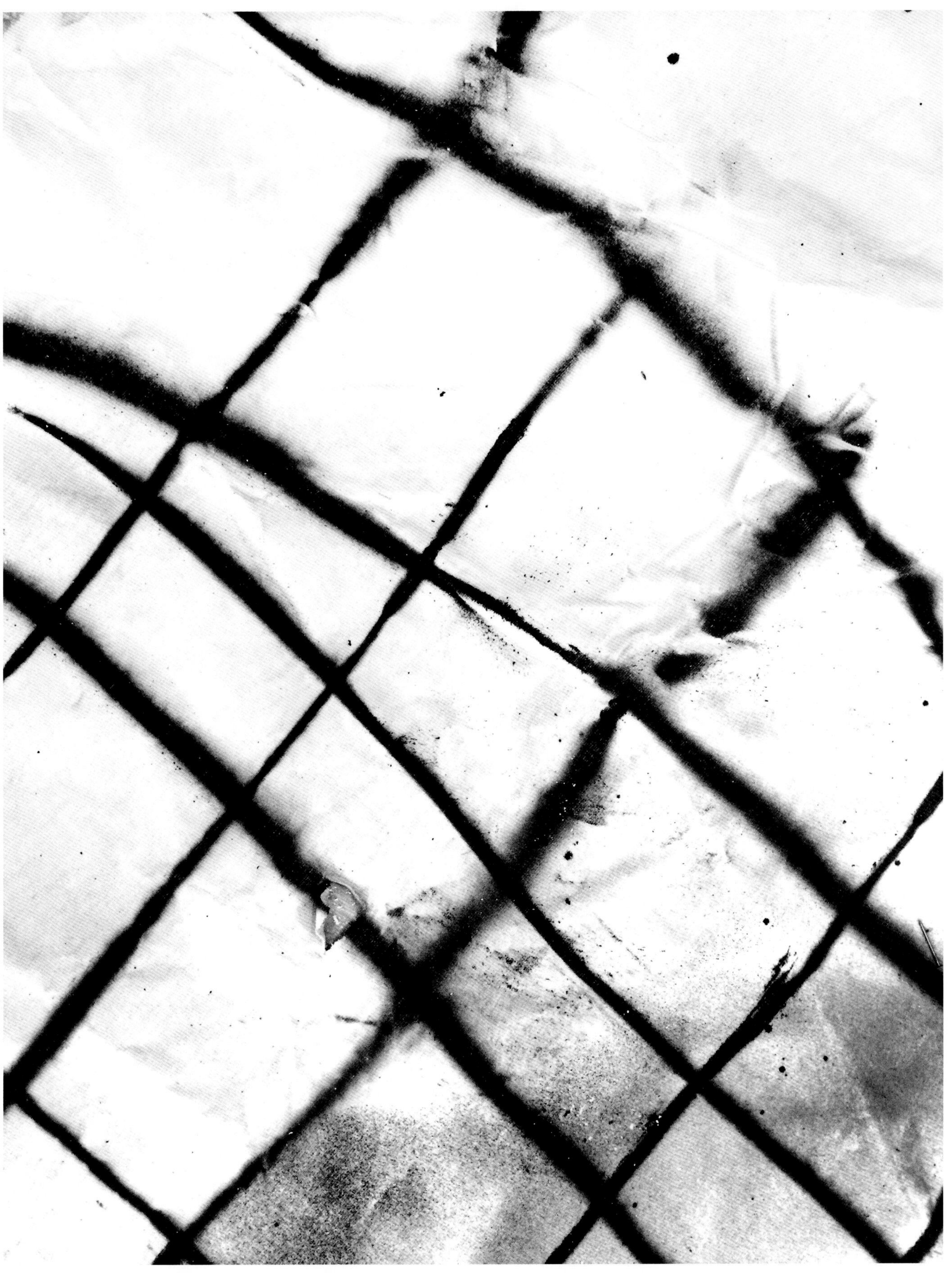

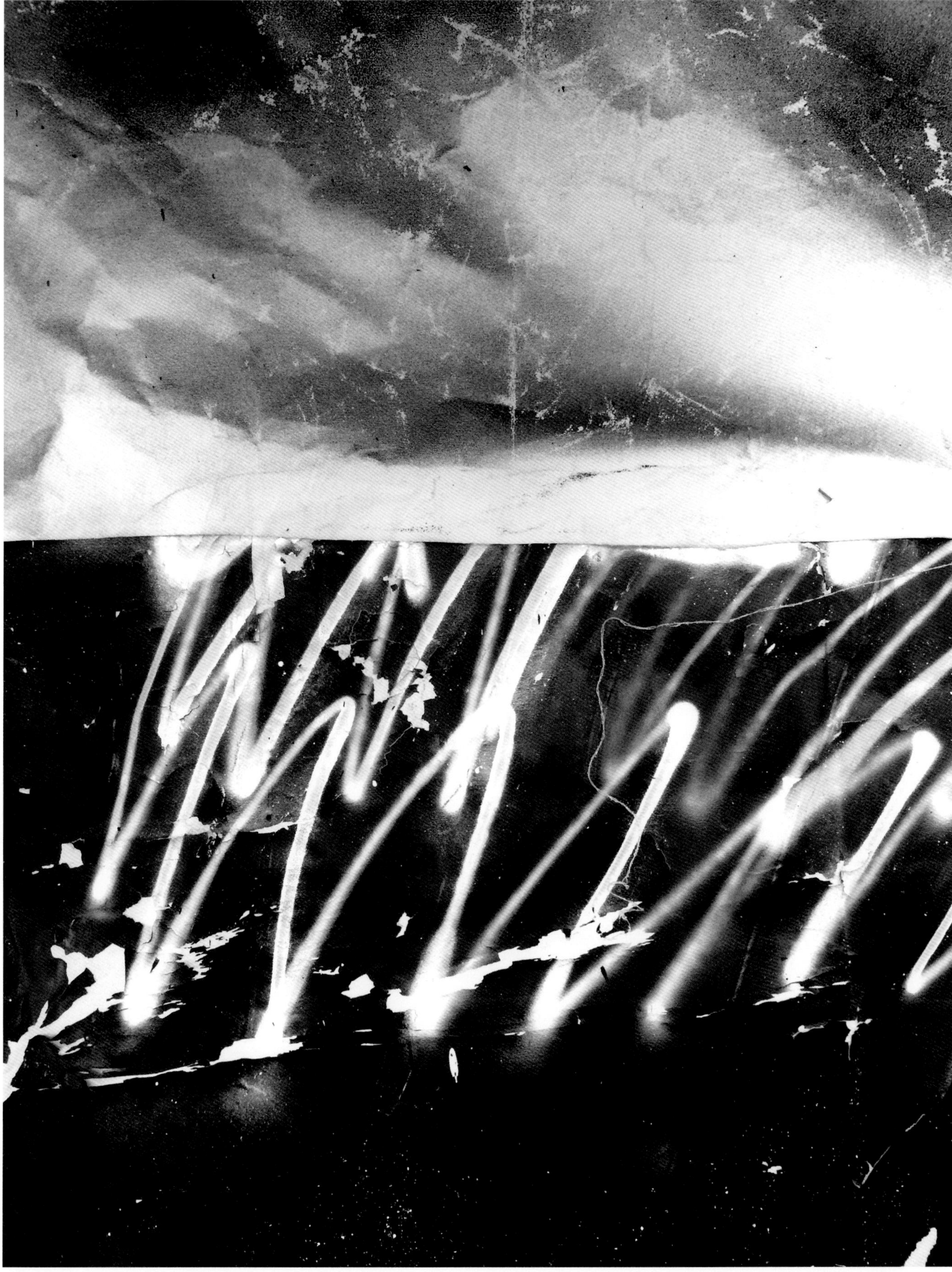

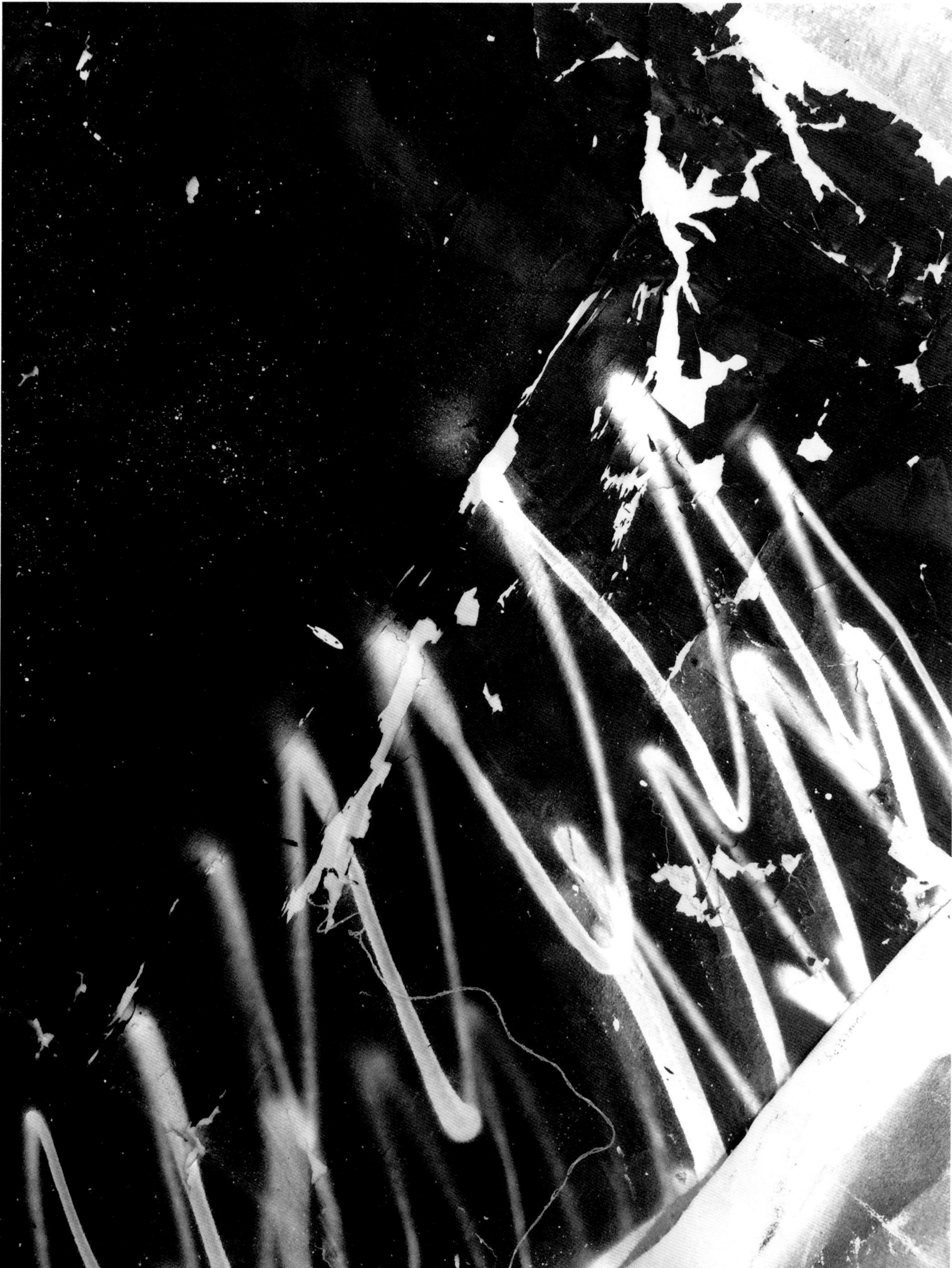

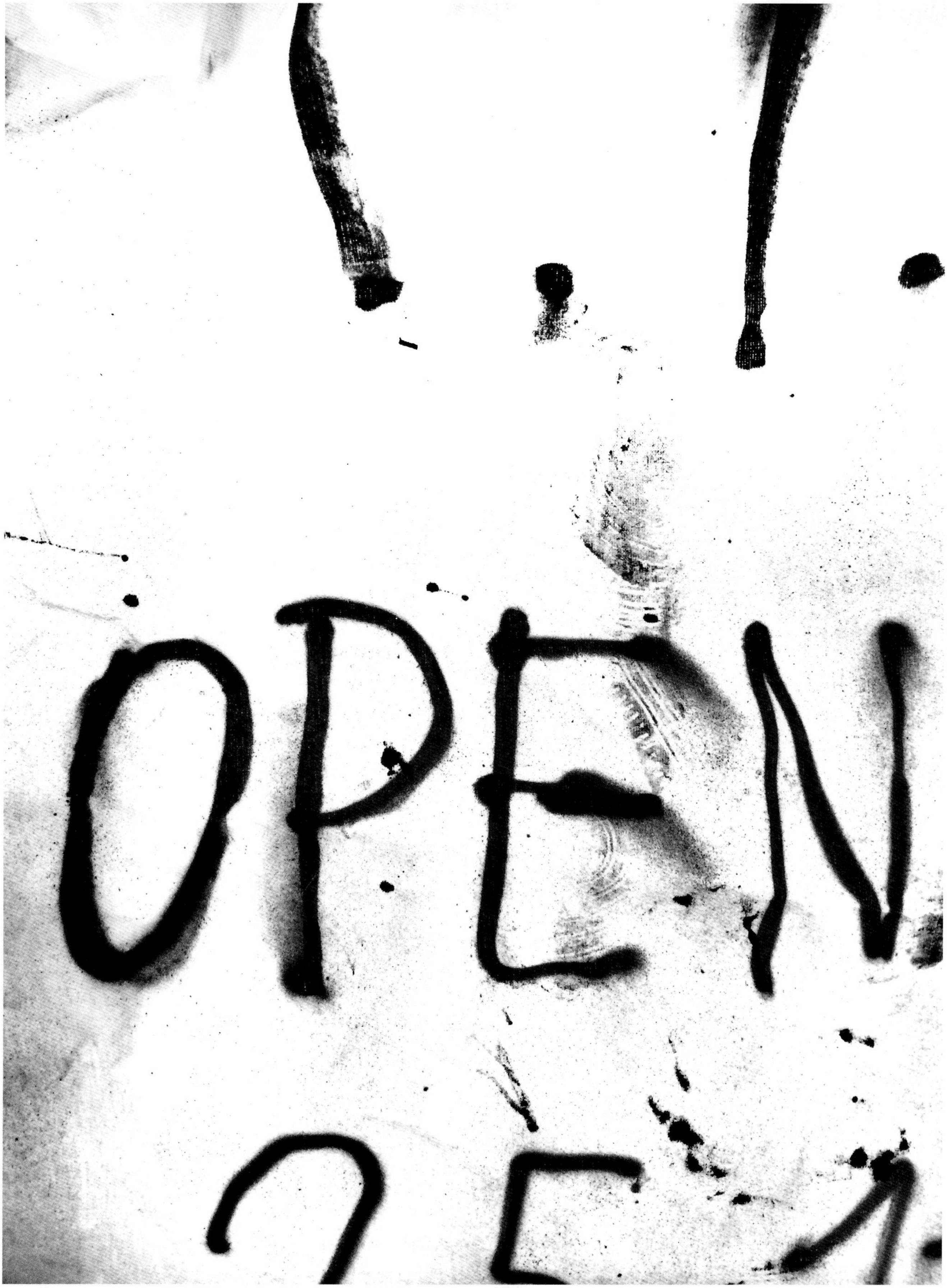

!.!.

OPEN

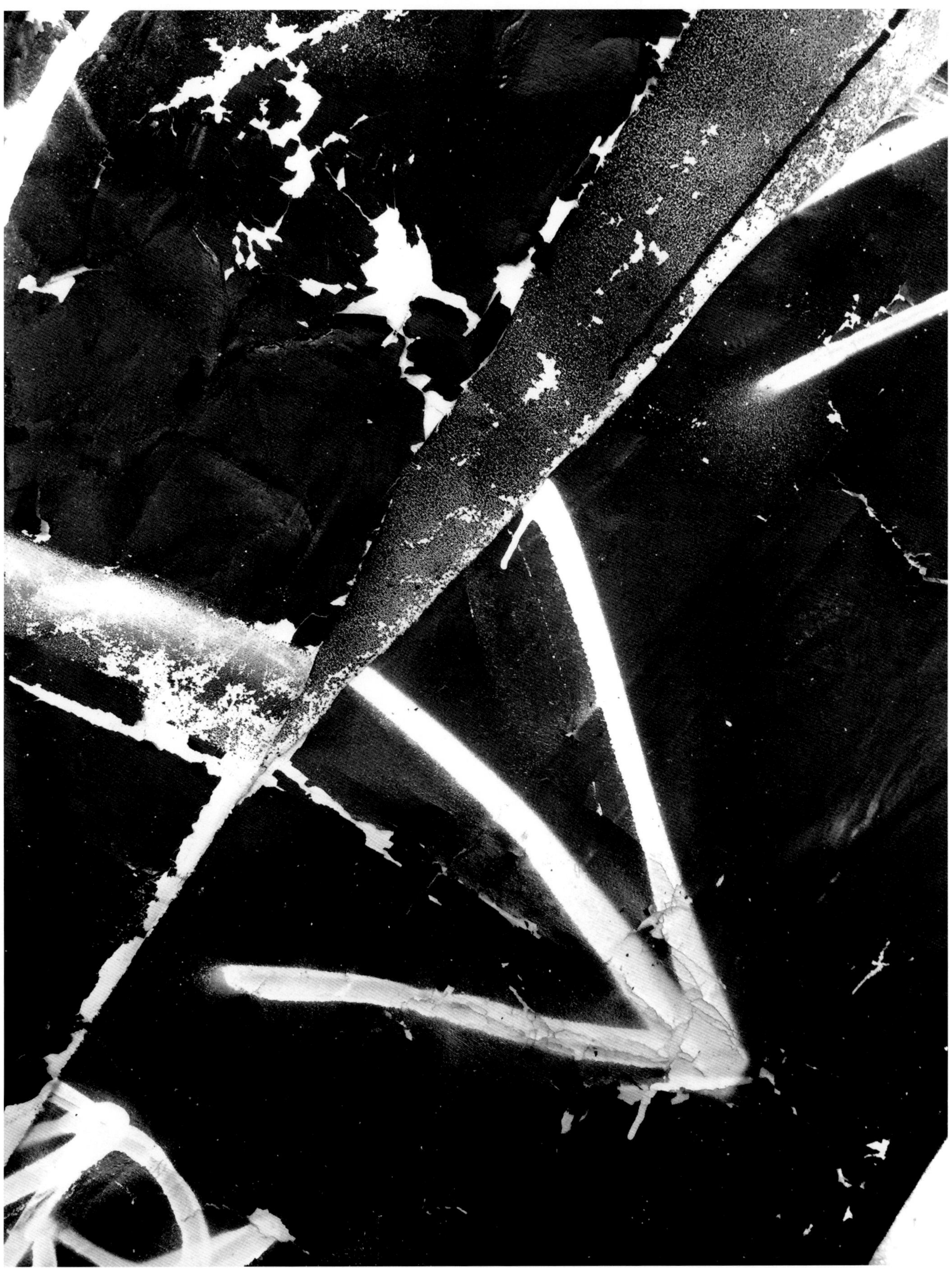

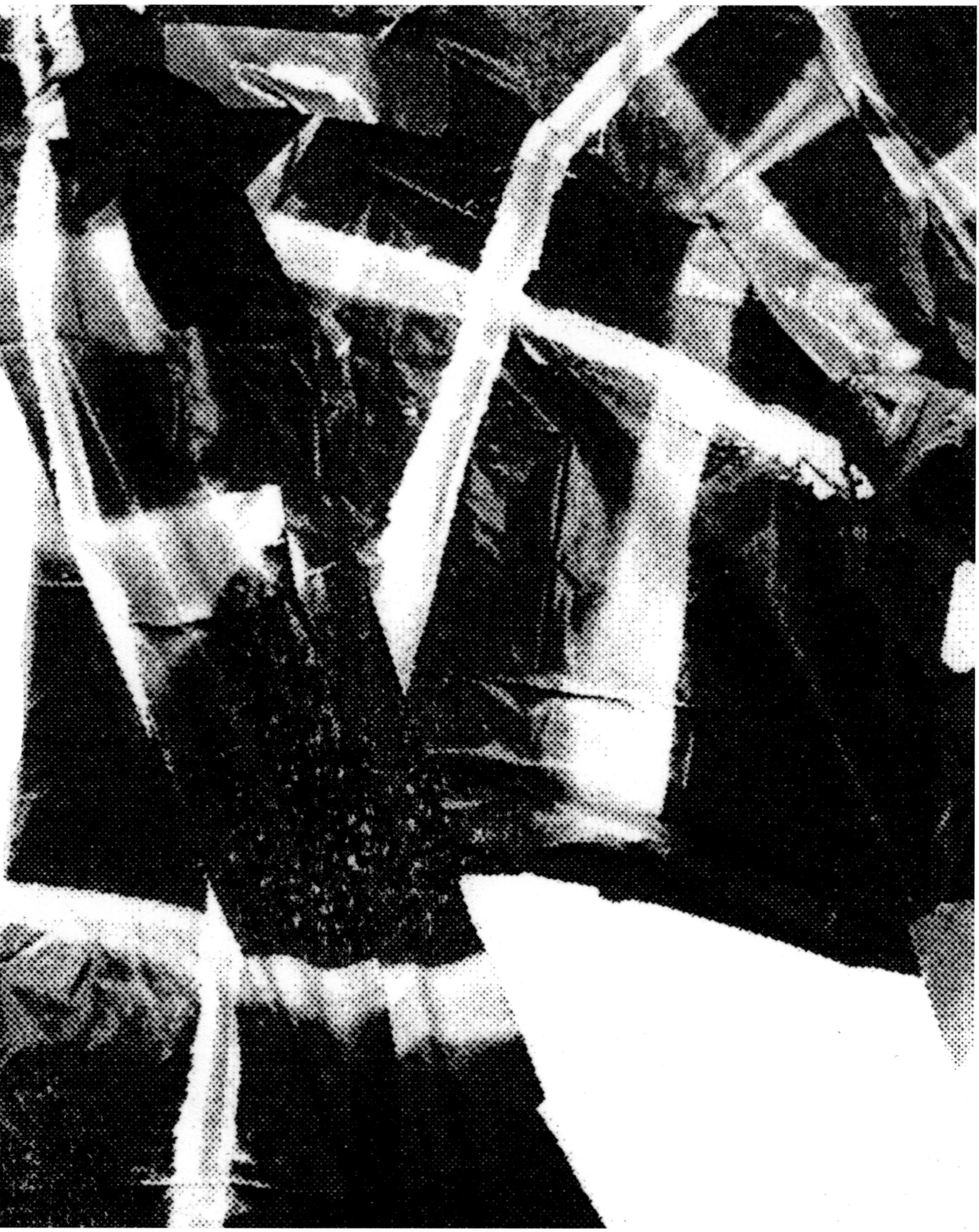

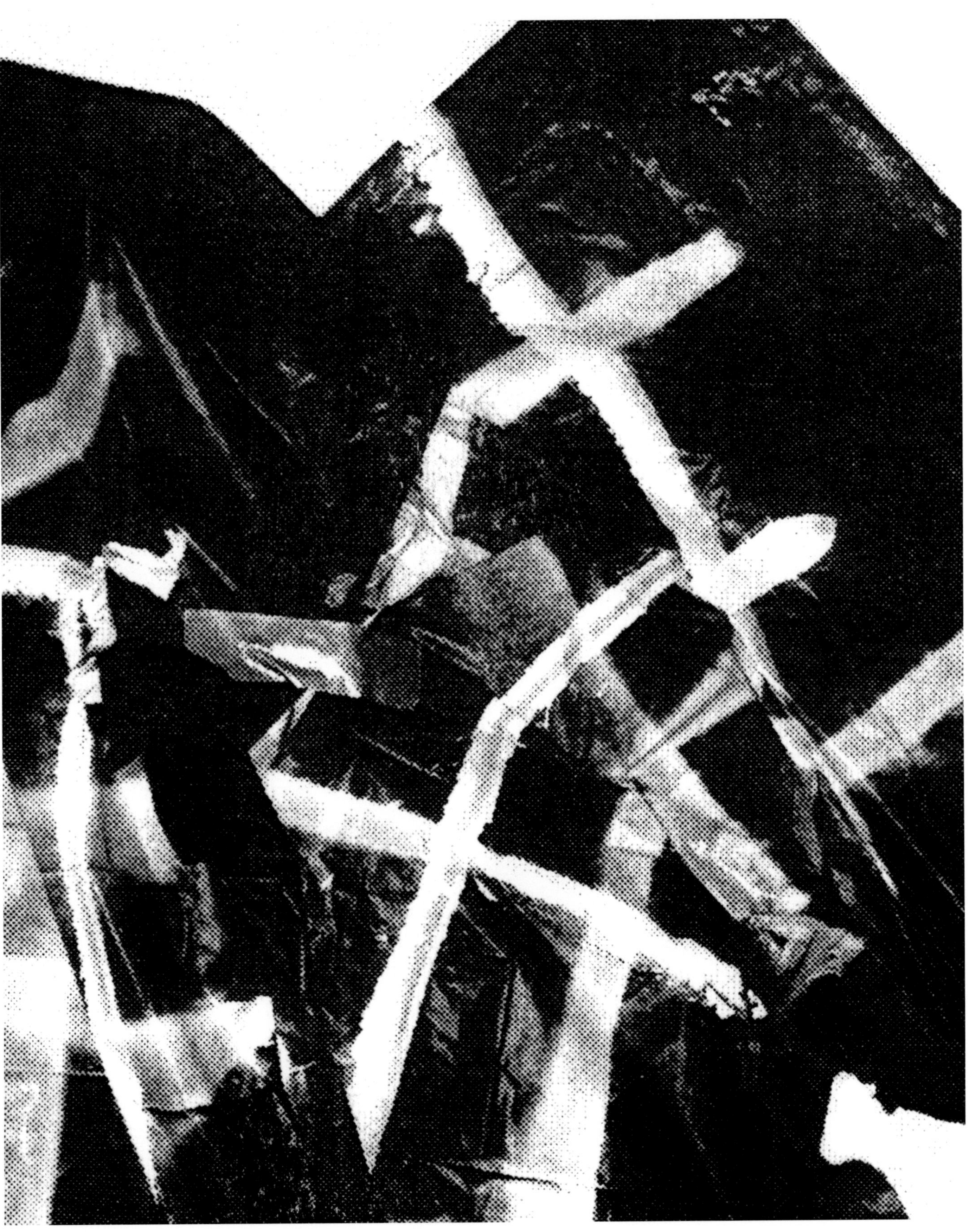

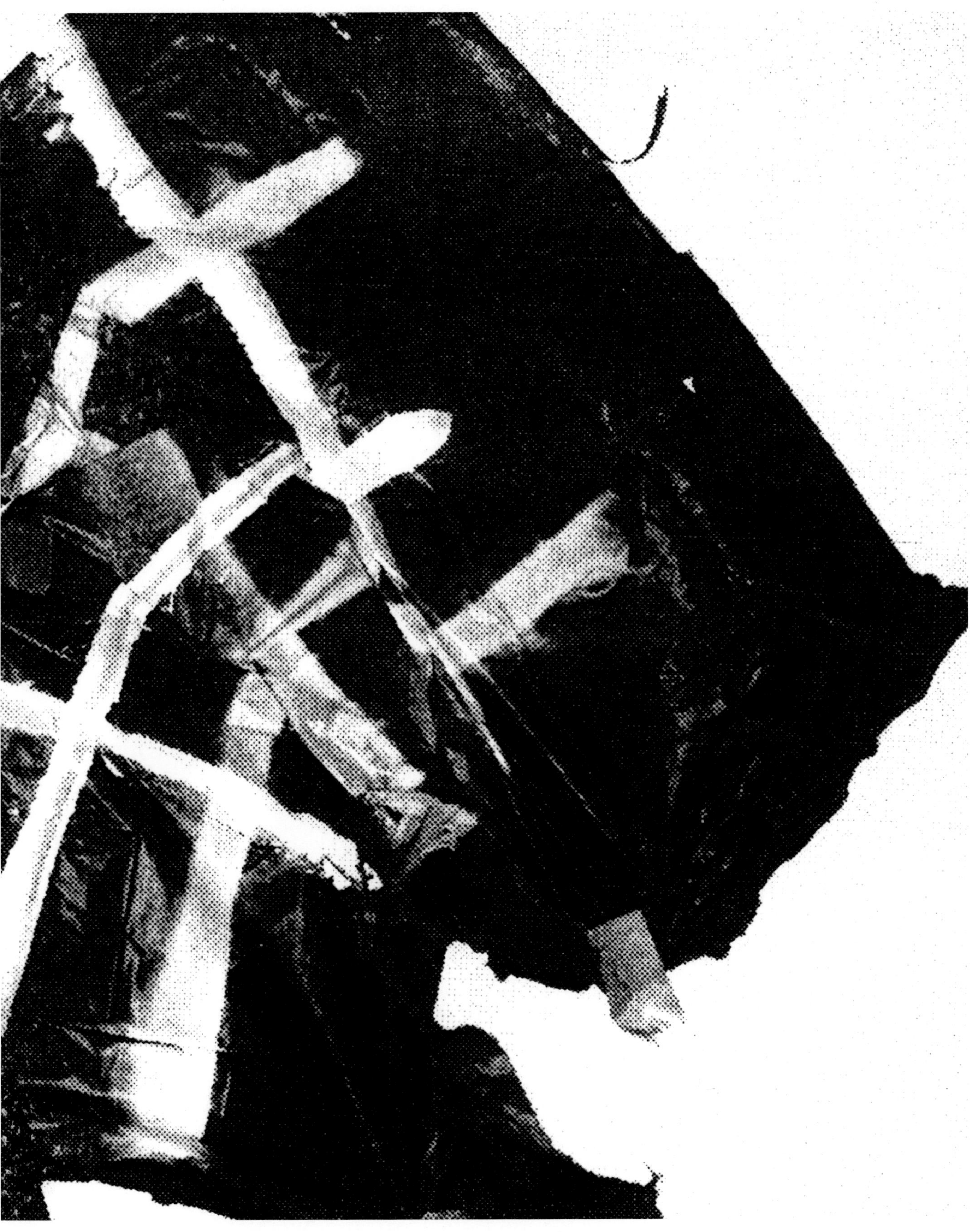

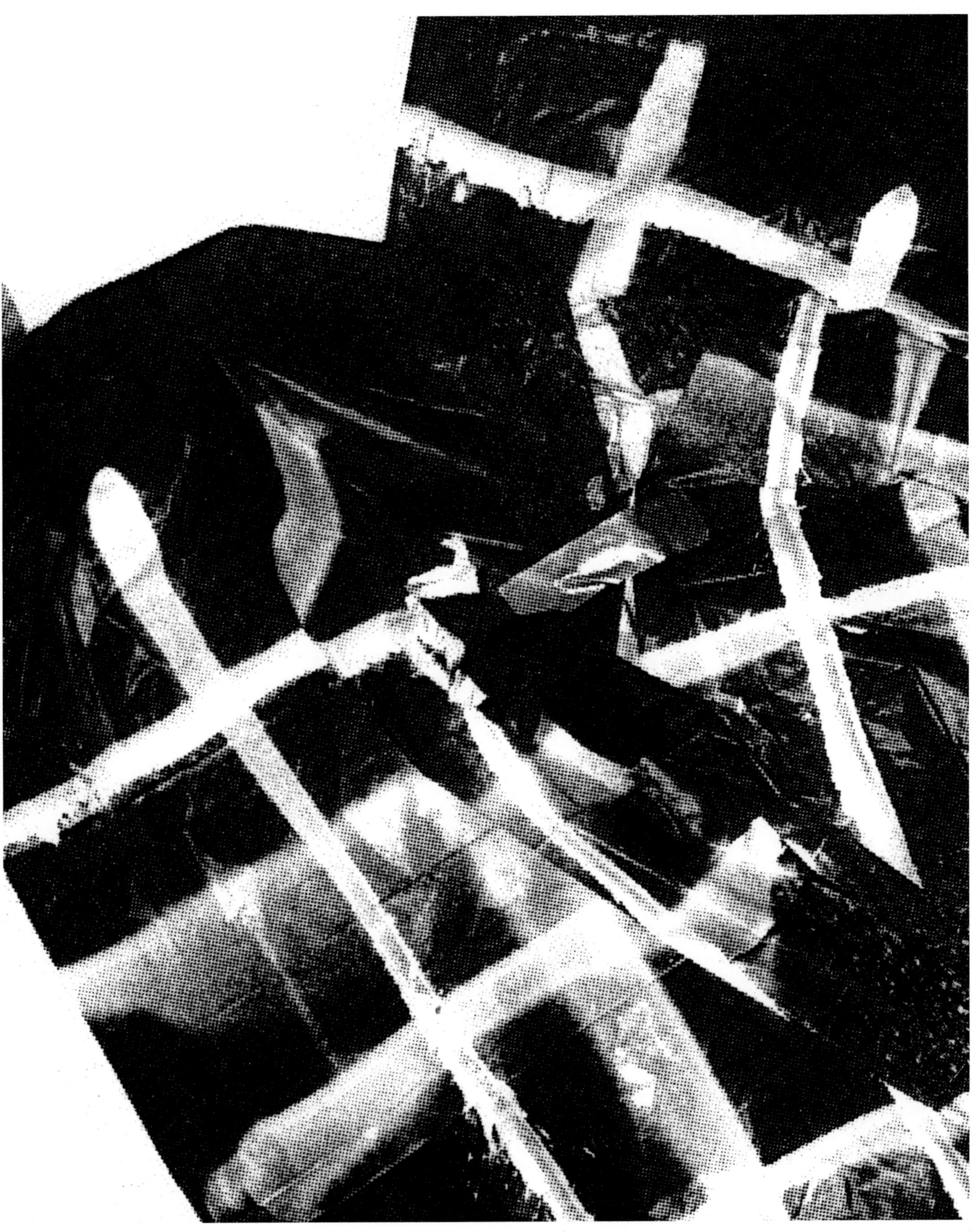

APE#055
Philippe Van Wolputte
Temporary Penetrable Exhibition Spaces

ISBN 9789490800352
www.artpapereditions.org
www.vanwolputteprogress.eu
First edition of 500 copies

Graphic design: Jurgen Maelfeyt
Texts: Eric Fredericksen, Sandra Smets, Pieter Vermeulen
Editing: Mia Verstraete
Printing: New Goff, Ghent
Distribution: Idea Books, www.ideabooks.nl

With the support of the Flemish governement.

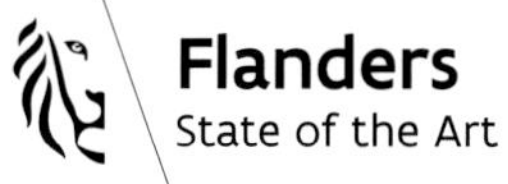

Thanks to: Bruthaus Gallery, Guillaume Bijl, Jenny Chert, Levy Delval, Laurence Dujardin, Eric Fredericksen, Lode Geens, Bart Geernaert, Chris Gillis, Petrit Halilaj, Mies Harleman, Harry Heirmans, Laurent Jacobs, Chiaki Kato, Nico Köppe, Wilfried Lentz, Mark Luyten, Rufus Mich, Olivier Robichon, Silvio Salgado, Sandra Smets, Maite Smeyers, Marc Swysen, Koen Theys, Adrien Tirtiaux, Alvaro Urbano, Walt Van Beeck, Kerlijn Van Der Cruyssen, Pieter Vermeulen.